To:

_____

From:

_____

THE CASE FOR

Hope

LEE STROBEL

ZONDERVAN®

The Case for Hope
Copyright © 2015 by Lee Strobel

Requests for information should be addressed to:

Zondervan, Grand Rapids, Michigan 49530

ISBN: 978-0-310-33957-1

Special thanks to Mark Mittelberg for his invaluable contribution to creating this book.

Cover design by Jeff and Lisa Franke, Art Lab Studios
Cover photo by Vladimir Piskunov, Getty Images

Printed in China

15 16 17 18 19 20 /TIMS/ 22 21 20 19 18 17 16 15 14 13 12 11 10 9 8 7 6 5 4 3 2 1

Contents

CHAPTER ONE

Finding Hope in a Hopeless World

These three remain: faith, hope and love.

1 CORINTHIANS 13:13

FAITH, HOPE, AND LOVE. ACCORDING TO THE BIBLE THESE are three indispensable and eternally enduring commodities, ones we ultimately can't live without.

Love, said Jesus, is the driving principle behind God's greatest commands. We must love God first, with everything we've got. And we must love our neighbors as we love ourselves (Matthew 22:34–40). It's no surprise that these are God's central values: the Bible tells us that at his very core "God *is* love" (1 John 4:8, 16, emphasis mine).

Faith, biblically defined, is trust in God and in the payment he made for our sins when Jesus died on the cross. The apostle Paul said, "For it is by grace you have been saved, through faith" (Ephesians 2:8). Grace is a blessing we have not earned—in this case the gift of salvation that Jesus purchased for us—but faith is the means of receiving that gift.

And *hope*—the subject of this book—is the sense of expectancy and optimism that God wants to instill in all of us who love him and have faith in him. It's an overriding confidence he gives, reminding us that, even in the midst of our greatest problems, God is still with us—and he is greater than any challenge we might face.

Hope is the inextinguishable flicker God ignites in our souls to keep us believing in the prevailing power of his light even when we are surrounded by utter darkness. It's the unswerving belief that better days are ahead, probably in this world and most certainly in the next. It's the quiet resolve he hardwires into our spirit that clings to the seemingly impossible truth that "in all things God works for the good of those who love him" and that, in the grand scheme of things, "we are more than conquerors through him who loved us" (Romans 8:28, 37).

It was the apostle Paul—that unsinkable carrier of

divine hope—who proclaimed, "For I am convinced that neither death nor life, neither angels nor demons, neither the present nor the future, nor any powers, neither height nor depth, nor anything else in all creation, will be able to separate us from the love of God that is in Christ Jesus our Lord" (Romans 8:38–39).

That, my friend, is a great reason for our hope, a truth that we need to let soak into our very being, because we live in a culture that seems bent on spreading, with evangelistic zeal, its relentless message of complete hopelessness.

Maybe that message has been getting the best of you. Perhaps your future feels uncertain, or a sense of guilt from your past weighs you down. Problems never seem far away.

"In this world you will have trouble," Jesus warned. "But take heart! I have overcome the world" (John 16:33).

We must, with God's help, learn to cling to that rare and wonderful thing called hope. Otherwise, we're destined for despair.

A CASE STUDY IN HOPELESSNESS

Major Harold Kushner was a prisoner of the Viet Cong for more than five years. Kushner describes one of his fellow

American prisoners, a tough twenty-four-year-old Marine who had made a deal with their captors. The Marine agreed to cooperate with the enemy, and in return the commander of the prison camp promised he would let him go.

The young Marine did whatever was asked of him. He became a model prisoner, and he even became the leader of the camp's thought-reform group. But before long it became clear to him that the camp commander had lied to him and that the Viet Cong had no intention of actually releasing him.

This is how Major Kushner described what happened next to the Marine: "When the full realization of this took hold, he became a zombie. He refused to do all the work, and he rejected all offers of food and encouragement. He simply lay on his cot, sucking his thumb. In a matter of weeks, he was dead."[1]

The cause of this prisoner's death might be summarized in one word: *hopelessness.*

There's little doubt that hopelessness can kill. In World War II, Korea, and Vietnam, many prisoners died from a condition doctors nicknamed "give-up-itis." The prisoners faced grim conditions and had no apparent prospect of freedom, and some of them became demoralized and deeply mired in despair. After a while they turned apathetic. They refused to eat or drink. They spent their time staring blankly into space. Drained of hope, these prisoners gradually wasted away and died.

The human spirit needs hope to survive and thrive. Said Dr. Arnold Hutschnecker, "Since my early years as a physician, I learned that taking away hope is, to most people, like pronouncing a death sentence. Their already hard-pressed will to live can become paralyzed, and they may give up and die."[2]

The Bible set forth the essential nature of hope almost three thousand years ago, when King Solomon wrote in Proverbs 13:12: "Hope deferred makes the heart sick, but a longing fulfilled is a tree of life."

Pollster George Gallup observed, "People in many nations appear to be searching with a new intensity for spiritual moorings. One of the key factors prompting this search is a need for hope in these troubled times."[3]

It's not surprising that if God created us with a craving for hope, he would also serve as our ultimate Source of hope. Romans 15:13 refers to him as "the God of hope." In fact, the Bible is a book brimming with hope. All told, there are ninety-seven uses of the word *hope* in the Old Testament and another eighty-three in the New Testament. The theme of hope is woven throughout Scripture.

God offers a hope so powerful that it can transform a person's life and rewrite a person's future. But it's not the kind of hope we usually think of when we use that word. In fact, we use the term all the time to mean different things. Much of what we call "hope" falls into three categories: *wishful thinking, blind optimism,* and *hopeful dreams.*

WISHFUL THINKING

Wishful thinking is when we try to change reality with our thoughts, attempting to hope things into or out of existence. It's when we blow out the candles on our birthday cake and say to ourselves, "I hope I stay healthy for another year." It's when we pick up the *Wall Street Journal* and say, "I hope my stocks have gone up again." Or it's when we turn on the TV and say, "I hope our team beats the visiting team!"

Wishful thinking is an almost superstitious feeling that maybe, somehow, some way, our sincere desires will help things go the direction we want them to, even though we really don't have any power to make them happen.

Sometimes we engage in wishful thinking so much that we begin to convince ourselves that something's true even though it isn't. For example, years ago Leslie was

Hope is the inextinguishable flicker
God ignites in our souls to keep us
believing in the prevailing power
of his light even when we are
surrounded by utter darkness.

pregnant with our first child, and I really wanted to have a boy. So I kept thinking about the baby being a boy. I even picked out boy's names. My desire for a boy was so strong that I became increasingly convinced we would soon have our son.

Finally the delivery day came. No kidding! I was there in the room, and the doctor delivered this beautiful baby girl. He held her up, I looked at her for the first time, and I exuberantly exclaimed: "It's a boy!"

Looking at me like I was a sex-education dropout, the doctor said, "Guess again!"

I had convinced myself that the baby was going to be a boy, but obviously that belief did nothing to affect the outcome. Of course we soon found out how great it was to have a girl like Alison, so then the second time around we were wishing for another daughter. Once again our wishes had no influence, and we soon had our second child, a wonderful little boy named Kyle.

The lesson? Wishful thinking doesn't change reality.

BLIND OPTIMISM

Another hopeful attitude is blind optimism. It's good to have a positive outlook, but some optimists are prone to seeing everything through rose-colored glasses. They paper over their problems as if those problems don't exist; they avert their eyes from the ugly aspects of the world; they act as if, for them, everything will be fine *all* the time.

There's a story about the parents of two young sons. One boy was a terrible pessimist, the other, an incessant optimist. The parents were worried because each son's personality was quite extreme. So at Christmastime the father said to his wife, "We need to do something drastic to break these boys out of their molds."

The parents filled up the pessimist's room with dozens and dozens of brand-new toys, and they filled up the optimist's room from floor to ceiling with horse manure, hoping this would help moderate their sons' attitudes.

Christmas morning finally came. The children were in their rooms for a couple of hours, and then the pessimist finally came out. The father asked him, "Did you play with your new toys?"

The pessimist moaned, "Nah, I didn't take them out of their packages. I was afraid that if I touched them, they'd just break, and then I'd be disappointed."

Then the optimist came bounding out of his room that had been filled with horse manure, and he was all smiles. His dad asked, "Why are you so happy?"

"I just know that if I keep digging long enough," replied the boy, "I'm going to find that pony!"

Do you know people like that? Optimists who are convinced everything's always great, who gloss over problems in their lives? Their positive attitude might seem admirable, but, again, it doesn't change reality.

HOPEFUL DREAMS

Then there are hopeful dreams. These are the lofty goals that we choose for ourselves and set out to achieve. In other words, we don't just wish for a new car; we begin saving for one. We don't just wish we could become a better golfer; we take lessons and spend time on the practice tee. We don't just wish for a good marriage; we work at improving communication with our spouse.

Now, that's all fine, and taking steps toward achievement can be very helpful. But the problem is that our hopeful dreams are restricted by our limitations. I could fantasize, for example, about becoming the next big NBA star, and I could even begin perfecting my free throw. But that wouldn't change the fact that my vertical leap has to be measured in millimeters! There's no way I'm ever going to get recruited by the Los Angeles Lakers. There are simply too many limitations—my age, physique, talent, and health—to make that a realistic possibility.

Also, our dreams often fall victim to other factors that are beyond our control. For instance, most corporate workers hope for lifelong job security and eventual retirement, but that doesn't stop companies from firing employees during economic downturns. Often the fulfillment of our hopeful dreams is at the mercy of others. Dwell on them as we might, our earnest belief in our dreams does not guarantee they will ever become a reality.

BIBLICAL HOPE

Now let me contrast wishful thinking, blind optimism, and hopeful dreams with biblical hope, which is the kind of hope described throughout Scripture. You see, for most people, hope is something they *do*, but the Bible talks about hope as something we can *have*.

Biblical hope is the confident expectation that God is willing and able to fulfill the promises he has made to those who trust in him. The Bible refers to this as "living hope," and it is directly linked to the work of Christ on our behalf. The apostle Peter wrote this: "In [God's] great mercy he has given us new birth into a living hope through the resurrection of Jesus Christ from the dead, and into an inheritance that can never perish, spoil or fade. This inheritance is kept in heaven for you" (1 Peter 1:3–4).

As we'll explore in the next chapter, Jesus demonstrated through his resurrection that he really is God and that he truly does possess the power to fulfill his promises to us.

Promises that he'll change our life.

Promises that he'll guide us.

Promises that he'll cause good to emerge from our personal problems.

Promises that he'll grant us eternal life.

The resurrection is an actual, physical event in history that sealed Jesus' identity as God Incarnate, who loves us and is committed to helping us.

Hebrews 6:19 says, "We have this hope as an anchor for the soul, firm and secure." Now, I hate being on boats, so I don't like to use boating illustrations. I usually have to wear a seasick patch just to talk about the subject, but an anchor really is a great analogy. That's because our hope is only as good as whatever we anchor it to.

In and of itself, hope doesn't have the power to change reality. We hope for this, we hope for that, and we might feel better for awhile. We might fool ourselves into thinking that everything will be okay.

But the only way hope has any impact is when we anchor it to the One who has real power. And not only does he have power, but he also has the strong desire to help. Anchoring our hope to Christ means we live with a confident expectation that he will therefore fulfill his promises to us.

Since I began following Christ, I've increasingly experienced that kind of hope. In fact, I want to discuss two important areas where I've drawn hope from him. I'm confident these areas will be encouraging to you as well.

ABSOLVED OF OUR PAST

First, there's hope because I've been absolved of my past. The Bible says in Lamentations 3:21–23, "This I call to mind and therefore I have hope: Because of the LORD's great love we are not consumed, for his compassions never fail. They are new every morning."

In other words, we can live with hope because even though we fail God, fail our families, and fail ourselves, God's compassion is a renewable resource. It's fresh and available every day, and he's willing to offer us a new start.

I was thinking about this while I was watching the comedy *City Slickers*. Do you remember that film? It's about three guys from New York City who were in various stages of midlife crisis, so they decided to break out of their familiar settings and head out West on an adventure vacation that included riding horses on a cattle drive. This gave them lots of time to talk about their lives.

One of the guys was named Phil, and his life was a wreck. He was in a dead-end job at his father-in-law's grocery store, and he was facing a divorce. In one scene, he and his buddies were in a tent when Phil broke down and began crying.

"I'm at a dead end!" he sobbed. "I'm almost forty years old. I've wasted my life!"

One of his friends tried to console him. "But now you've got a chance to start over," he said. "Remember when we were kids and we'd be playing ball and the ball would get stuck up in the tree or something? We'd yell, '*Do-over!*' Look, Phil, your life is a do-over. You've got a clean slate!"

But Phil wasn't so sure. "I've got no place to live. I'm going to get wiped out in the divorce because I've committed adultery, so I may never even see my kids again. I'm alone!" he said. "How's that slate look now?"

As I watched that scene, I thought, *How is a guy like*

Phil ever going to really be able to start over? And the answer is only through the kind of do-over he can get from God. After all, God is in the do-over business! He's the one who offers us a new birth (John 3:3), who proclaims "the new creation has come: The old has gone, the new is here!" (2 Corinthians 5:17), and who finally declares, "I am making everything new!" (Revelation 21:5).

We can wish we'd never committed the wrongs that we've committed. We can attempt to cover them up as if they never really happened. We can try to deal with them on our own. But Jesus would tell us, "I can erase your sins so you can truly start over. I can forgive you, and I can help you heal and find hope again."

Some people need a do-over from God because guilt has squeezed the hope out of their lives. This is what had happened to a woman who wrote a letter to our church. Several years earlier she had been living with a man, and she got pregnant. Even though she wanted the baby very much, her boyfriend persuaded her to have an abortion. Then, later, he abandoned her.

The woman wrote, "For years I was miserable. I was ashamed of myself for not being strong enough to stand up for myself or my baby."

Do you see how guilt tries to convince us that our

The only way hope has any impact is when we anchor it to the One who has real power.

failures disqualify us from ever starting over? Guilt robs us of hope.

Remorse haunted this young woman for years. Finally, in desperation, she turned to Christ and, in effect, asked for a do-over, for a fresh start from God. He not only forgave her and wiped her slate clean, but he has healed her emotions as well.

Now that God's forgiveness has renewed her hope, it's like the darkness has been lifted and a new day has dawned. This is what she wrote before she was baptized as a follower of Jesus: "I can't thank God enough for all the grace I received from him." She later declared through her baptism that this God who had given her a new beginning is the God she wants to follow and serve forever.

How about you? Is it time to ask God for a do-over in your life? If you're lugging around a backpack filled with guilt over mistakes you've made, a marriage that went bad, kids you've let down, or promises to God that you've broken, don't keep carrying your past—whatever it is—into your future.

The question is not "Will God grant you a do-over?" The Bible promises, "If we confess our sins, he is faithful and just and will forgive us our sins and purify us from all unrighteousness" (1 John 1:9). God is anxious to give you a do-over; the question is whether you're willing to reach out and ask for one.

Or maybe you can relate to Phil's character in *City Slickers* because you're realizing that, like him, you've been wasting your life. You've pursued your own hopes and dreams long enough to accumulate a bunch of stuff that, in the end, has failed to satisfy your soul.

A successful executive sat across from me at lunch and told me how empty he felt despite all he had achieved in his business. There's nothing wrong with what he had accomplished, but he said to me, "I've been a casual Christian all my life, and I'm sick to death of it." He almost spit out the words. "It's a boring and frustrating life, and I want to stop, but I don't know what to do."

I'll tell you what I told him: it's not too late for a do-over. To say to God, "I don't want to squander my one and only life any longer. Let me start over, and this time I'll keep my compass pointed in your direction. I want to experience the adventure of being your follower. I want to feel the exhilaration of having a mission in life that really matters. I want my life to add up to something more than just a bunch of material things."

God is the God of do-overs, and that should give us great hope. We really *can* be absolved of our past.

Hope for Our Future

Second, we can have hope because we can be assured of our future.

Sometimes I think back to the days when I was convinced there was no God. I would lie awake at night and think about the ultimate hopelessness of life. I believed that when we die, that's it. *Lights out.* There's nothing more.

That's a terrifying thought, isn't it? About one out of four Americans thinks that death is the end of their human existence,[4] and that idea breeds hopelessness—a hopelessness so dark that many can't face it, so they revert to false forms of hope. They engage in wishful thinking: "Maybe when I die, I'll be reincarnated or something." Or they leap into blind optimism: "I just won't think about it. By the time I get around to dying, they'll have a cure for whatever I've got." Others pursue hopeful dreams by saying, "I'll watch my carbs, run the treadmill, cut my weight, and lengthen my lifespan."

Those defense mechanisms may make people feel better, but they don't change the reality that death still plays a perfect game: *one out of one ends up dead*. And death has an annoying habit of being completely unpredictable.

I was talking about the inevitability of death with a

computer salesman named Jeff Miller, who attended our church. He told me about a fateful flight he had taken from Denver to Chicago. About forty minutes before they were to land at O'Hare International Airport, there was a muffled explosion, and the plane swung to the side so violently that the book Jeff was reading flew out of his hands. As it turned out, the engine in the tail had exploded, and the plane's steering was severely crippled.

As the plane made the approach for an emergency landing in Sioux City, Iowa, it became clear that the situation was desperate. Jeff told me that some of the people around him began trembling and crying from fear. Others put on an air of optimism and kept telling themselves there was nothing to worry about. But Jeff, who had been a Christian for several years, spent the time praying a simple prayer that was anchored in hope.

He said, "Thank you, Lord, that you're mine and I'm yours. God, I want to live, but I know if I don't, I'll be with you, and you'll care for my family." Jeff had a confident expectation that God would fulfill his promises to him.

You may have seen the video of that plane when it scraped awkwardly onto the runway, broke apart, cartwheeled, and exploded into orange flames. Jeff braced himself for a violent death, but it never came. His piece of the fuselage tumbled into a cornfield, where it came to a stop, upside down. Jeff hung there, suspended in his seat, with not a mark on him.

I asked Jeff, "What was it like when everyone knew the plane was going down? I mean, people don't usually survive airplane crashes. Was there a feeling of being in a hopeless situation?"

He said, "Lee, I'll tell you the truth. It *was* scary, but at the same time I felt like I was full of hope. I mean, there was hope if I lived, and there was the hope that if I died, I'd be with Christ. It's like it says in Psalm 118:6: 'What can anybody do to you if your hope is in the Lord.'"

HOPE IN A HOPELESS WORLD

How we face death tells us a lot about how we'll face life. The Bible says that because followers of Christ have the hope of eternity, they can live their lives with boldness and strength.

When you have the confident expectation that God will live up to his promises, it changes the way you think about death. I know it has for me.

When I was a fairly new Christian, I remember watching television one day, and they were featuring a world-class figure skater named Nancy Kerrigan of Boston. While she was skating, the camera showed her mother at the side of the rink with her nose pressed up against a large television set. Nancy's mom had been struck virtually blind when she was thirty-one years old, so she needed to get right up to the big screen to see anything.

The interviewer asked her what she was able to make out. She said, "Well, I can see some shapes and movement when she jumps." And then she broke down and started to cry. Between sobs, she said, "But I can't see her face! *I can't see my daughter's face!*"

Her words grabbed me. They helped me understand something I'd been feeling, because Mrs. Kerrigan's experience with her daughter was a little like my relationship with Christ. I've been able to sense his comfort in my life; I've experienced his presence; I've felt him guiding me and loving me. *But I can't see his face.*

Yet I have the confident expectation that one day I'll stand before him, and at that moment I'll finally be able to look straight into his eyes. That's not something to fear for those who know him; it's something to anticipate with excitement. God has taken me from a state of hopelessness about death to having real hope.

Let me encourage you to pray a prayer as you continue

reading this book. Say to God, "I want to know for certain, with your help, that I've been absolved of my past, and I want to be confident, through Christ, that I've been assured of my future."

My prayer is that, moving ahead, you'll base your hope not on wishful thinking or any of the other counterfeit versions, but on the One who has the power to truly change your life and assure your eternity.

Sacrificial Hope

Earlier in this chapter I told a story about a prisoner of war that illustrated how hopelessness can drain life from us. Now I want to end with another POW story, one that illustrates the hope we can have in Christ.

My friend, author and speaker Cliffe Knechtle, recounts the story of a group of Allied soldiers who were being held prisoner by the Japanese army during World War II. Each day, they were taken into a field to do hard labor. One day, at the end of their long shift, the guards counted the number of shovels and discovered that one was missing. They lined up the prisoners and said, "Who stole the shovel?"

Nobody stepped forward to confess. They again

demanded an answer, and nobody responded. With that, the commander shouted, "All die! All die!" The guards cocked their rifles and aimed at the prisoners' heads.

At that moment, all hope appeared lost. The men braced themselves for the bullets.

But before the triggers were pulled, a Scottish soldier stepped forward and said, "I stole the shovel." Instantly, the guards turned their guns on him and shot him dead.

The other soldiers carried his body and the remaining tools back to the prison camp. When they arrived there, the Japanese guards counted the shovels once more, and do you know what they discovered? *There was no shovel missing.* They had miscounted.

The innocent Scottish soldier had sacrificed his life so that his comrades could live.

That story serves as a rough metaphor for what Jesus Christ has done for us. The Bible says we're all in a hopeless situation. We've all violated God's laws in one way or another, and because of our sins, we deserve a severe penalty. That penalty is spiritual death, which is separation from God for all of eternity in a place of utter hopelessness.

That's the predicament we face, and no amount of wishful thinking, blind optimism, or hopeful dreaming can change it.

But because of his great love for you, Jesus Christ stepped forward to willingly take your death penalty so that you could be absolved of your past and assured of your future. And, frankly, the only reason we can have hope is because Jesus is saying, "All you need to do is trust in me and accept my payment on your behalf."

The all-important question is this: *What will your response be?*

As I close this chapter, let me point you to the hope-filled message of Ephesians 1:18–19:

> I pray that the eyes of your heart may be enlightened in order that you may know the hope to which he has called you, the riches of his glorious inheritance in his holy people, and his incomparably great power for us who believe.

CHAPTER TWO

The Source of Real Hope

*In his great mercy [God] has given us new birth into a living
hope through the resurrection of Jesus Christ from the dead.*
1 PETER 1:3

"WHERE IS THE HOPE?" ASKED CHRISTIAN STATESMAN
Chuck Colson. "I meet millions who tell me that they feel
demoralized by the decay around us. The hope that each
of us has is not in who governs us, or what laws are passed,
or what great things we do as a nation."[1]

Then where *is* the hope? In spite of how frequently
people banter about hope, this is still a challenging question. Colson pointed out that hope is not to be found in
government, laws, or a renewed sense of national pride.

And we've already seen that hope doesn't come from mere wishful thinking, blind optimism, or hopeful dreams. And, as it turns out, hope is an elusive commodity in most of the popular worldviews and religious options as well.

THE EMPTINESS OF ATHEISM

Atheism, for example, is bankrupt of ultimate hope. When you take God out of the equation, you're left with the belief that we got here by chance, we exist by accident, and we'll ultimately freeze up or flame out with the rest of the cosmos.

Renowned atheist Bertrand Russell said this about mankind:

> "His origin, his growth, his hopes and fears, his loves and his beliefs, are but the outcome of accidental col-locations of atoms . . . No fire, no heroism, no intensity of thought and feeling, can preserve individual life beyond the grave . . . All the labors of the ages, all the devotion, all the inspiration, all the noonday bright-ness of human genius, are destined to extinction in the vast death of the solar system . . . The whole temple of

man's achievement must inevitably be buried beneath the debris of a universe in ruins."[2]

Not very upbeat prospects for the skeptic!

In his article "Where Are the Honest Atheists?" Damon Linker, senior correspondent at *TheWeek.com*, said:

> "If atheism is true, it is far from being good news. Learning that we're alone in the universe, that no one hears or answers our prayers, that humanity is entirely the product of random events, that we have no more intrinsic dignity than non-human and even non-animate clumps of matter, that we face certain annihilation in death, that our sufferings are ultimately pointless, that our lives and loves do not at all matter in a larger sense, that those who commit horrific evils and elude human punishment get away with their crimes scot free—all of this (and much more) is utterly tragic."[3]

Religious Alternatives

Clearly, those seeking hope don't have much to relish in the atheistic worldview. But what about the religious alternatives? Do they offer genuine reasons for hope? Honestly, most of them don't fare much better than atheism.

Eastern religions such as Hinduism and Buddhism teach that we are morally defective beings who have created a huge debt of bad karma due to our negative behavior. We must, therefore, pay off our moral deficit over countless lifetimes as we successively are born, live our lives as best we can, die, and then come back as another reincarnated being in order to try to improve our record once again.

And we must do all of this even though our moral debts were incurred in past lifetimes through sinful acts we can't remember, and these debts must be paid in ways we can't measure.

In the case of Buddhism, the ultimate goal is to perfect ourselves over enough lifetimes that we can finally enter a state of Nirvana, a word that literally means "to extinguish." One Buddhist authority explained, "Nirvana is eternal. Because it is beyond space, there is no causation, no boundary, *no concept of self and not-self* and thus Nirvana is infinite."[4]

We're told that Nirvana is a place of great happiness,

but without the existence of a "self," it's hard to fathom who (or what?) would actually be able to enjoy that promised happiness. Buddhism seems to offer, at best, a fuzzy and futile form of hope.

And Islam offers a system of religion that depends on the faithfulness and good works of devout Muslims, with no assurance that in the end those works will measure up or be accepted by Allah. The Qur'an warns, for example, that "those whose scales are heavy [with good deeds]— it is they who are the successful. But those whose scales are light—those are the ones who have lost their souls, [being] in Hell, abiding eternally" (Qur'an 23:102–103).[5] But one can never know for certain in this life whether his or her scales are heavy or light.

Also, Allah is portrayed as aloof and often arbitrary in how he handles people: "Whoever Allah guides—he is the [rightly] guided; and whoever He sends astray—it is those who are the losers. . . . And if Allah had willed, He could have made you [of] one religion, but He causes to stray whom He wills and guides whom He wills. And you will surely be questioned about what you used to do" (Qur'an 7:178, 16:93).

In light of what atheism, Hinduism, Buddhism, and

Islam offer, I find myself returning to Chuck Colson's compelling question: *Where is the hope?*

THE SOURCE OF REAL HOPE

Thankfully, we have a good answer that is grounded not in wishful thinking, but in a historical event that gives us a solid reason to trust God for better things ahead, both in this life and the next. Specifically, I'm talking about the resurrection of Jesus.

If you read and reflect on the Gospel accounts about Jesus, you'll soon realize that he was a walking dispenser of hope! He lived a life that instilled in his followers the hope that they could find greater meaning and purpose in their lives. He spread tangible hope as he healed the broken hearts and diseased bodies of countless people. He embodied hope for our earthly lives, and he promised a hope-filled existence in heaven for eternity to those who would trust and follow him.

And when Jesus was challenged to explain the reasons for such hope, he staked it all on one imminent event: "Destroy this temple," he said, "and I will raise it again in three days." John explained in his gospel that the "temple [Jesus] had spoken of was his body" (John 2:19, 21). He was predicting not only his death, but also and especially his resurrection from the dead three days later.

So for Jesus' followers, both then and now, the Easter miracle is the make-or-break event. Either Jesus would rise from the dead, proving he was who he said he was and could do what he promised to do, or he would not, and he would be exposed as a fraud who was spreading false hope.

See why the resurrection is so important? That's why it's the lynchpin of Christianity. Said the apostle Paul: "If Christ has not been raised, your faith is futile; you are still in your sins . . . . If only for this life we have hope in Christ, we are of all people most to be pitied" (1 Corinthians 15:17, 19).

Thankfully, Paul didn't stop there! He went on to declare, *"But Christ has indeed been raised from the dead,* the firstfruits of those who have fallen asleep. For since death came through a man, the resurrection of the dead comes also through a man. For as in Adam all die, so in Christ all will be made alive" (1 Corinthians 15:20–22, emphasis mine).

The resurrection of Jesus is a powerful and miraculous event on which we can confidently pin our hopes—*but only if the resurrection actually happened.* So how can we really know that it is, indeed, supported by the persuasive evidence of history?

THE MINIMAL FACTS

This issue is so important that I'd like to invite you to pull up a chair and listen in on a conversation I had with Dr. Michael Licona, one of the world's leading scholars on the resurrection of Jesus.[6]

We discussed the details of what he and his mentor, Dr. Gary Habermas, call the "minimal facts case" for the resurrection, which they spell out in their book *The Case for the Resurrection of Jesus.*[7] I asked Licona to begin by explaining what they mean by a "minimal facts case."

"We only consider facts that meet two criteria," Licona said. "First, there must be very strong historical evidence supporting them. And, second, the evidence must be so strong that the vast majority of today's scholars on the subject—including skeptical ones—accept these as historical facts."

With that background in place, I issued Licona a challenge. "Use only the minimal facts," I said, "and let's see how strong of a case you can build for Jesus rising from the dead."

[Jesus] embodied hope for our earthly lives, and he promised a hope-filled existence in heaven for eternity to those who would trust and follow him.

Licona smiled and leaned forward in his chair. "I'll use just five minimal facts," he said, "and you can decide for yourself how persuasive the case is."

FACT #1: Jesus was killed by crucifixion.

"The first fact is Jesus' crucifixion," Licona began. "Even an extreme liberal like John Dominic Crossan says, 'That [Jesus] was crucified is as sure as anything historical ever can be.'[8] Skeptic James Tabor says, 'I think we need have no doubt that given Jesus' execution by Roman crucifixion he was truly *dead*.'[9] Both Gerd Lüdemann, who's an atheistic New Testament critic, and Bart Ehrman, who's an agnostic scholar, call the crucifixion an indisputable fact. Why? First of all, because all four Gospels report it [Matthew 27, Mark 15, Luke 23, and John 19].

"Now, beyond the four Gospels," Licona continued, "we also have a number of non-Christian sources that corroborate the crucifixion. For instance, the historian Tacitus said Jesus 'suffered the extreme penalty during the reign of Tiberius.' The Jewish historian Josephus reported that Pilate 'condemned him to be crucified.' Lucian of Samosata, who was a Greek satirist, mentioned the crucifixion, and Mara Bar-Serapion, who was a pagan, confirmed Jesus was executed. Even the Jewish Talmud reports that 'Yeshu was hanged.'"

"Yeshu? Hanged?" I asked.

"Yes, *Yeshu* is *Joshua* in Hebrew; the Greek equivalent is translated as *Jesus*. And in the ancient world, to be hung on a tree many times referred to a crucifixion. Galatians 3:13, for example, connects Jesus' crucifixion with the Pentateuch, which says that 'anyone who is hung on a tree is under God's curse'" [Deuteronomy 21:23].

"What were the odds of surviving crucifixion?" I asked.

"Extremely small. You saw *The Passion of the Christ*, right? Even though not all of the film was historically accurate, it did depict the extreme brutality of Roman scourging and crucifixion. Witnesses in the ancient world reported victims being so severely whipped that their intestines and veins were laid bare. As I said, Tacitus referred to it as 'the extreme penalty.' Cicero called it 'cruel and disgusting'— so horrendous that, he said, 'the very word *cross* should be far removed not only from the person of a Roman citizen but from his thoughts, his eyes, and his ears.'"

"We're dealing with a pretty primitive culture," I observed. "Were they competent enough to be sure that Jesus was dead?"

"I'm confident they were. You've got Roman soldiers carrying out executions all the time. It was their job. They were very good at it. Besides, death by crucifixion was basically a slow and agonizing demise by asphyxiation, because of the difficulty in breathing created by the victim's position on the cross. And that's something you can't fake.

"Lee, this first fact is as solid as anything in ancient history: Jesus was crucified and died as a result. The scholarly consensus—again, even among those who are skeptical toward the resurrection—is absolutely overwhelming. To deny it would be to take a marginal position that would get you laughed out of the academic world."

With that firmly established, Licona advanced to his next minimal fact.

FACT #2: Jesus' disciples believed that he rose and appeared to them.

"The second fact is the disciples' beliefs that Jesus had actually returned from the dead and had appeared to them," Licona said. "There are three strands of evidence for this: Paul's testimony about the disciples; oral traditions that passed through the early church; and the written works of the early church.

"Paul is important because he reported knowing

some of the disciples personally, including Peter, James, and John. Acts confirms this [Acts 9:26–30; 15:1–35]. And Paul said in 1 Corinthians 15:11 that whether 'it was I or they, this is what we preach,' referring to the resurrection of Jesus. So, in other words, Paul knew the apostles and reports that they claimed—just as he did—that Jesus had returned from the dead.

"Then we have oral tradition. Obviously, people in those days didn't have tape recorders and few people could read, so they relied on verbal transmission to pass along what happened until it was later written down. Scholars have identified several places in which this oral tradition has been copied into the New Testament in the form of creeds, hymns, and sermon summations. This is really significant because the oral tradition must have existed prior to the New Testament writings for the New Testament authors to have included them."

"So they're early."

"Very early, which weighs heavily in their favor, as any historian will tell you. For example, we have creeds that laid out basic doctrines in a form that was easily memorized. One of the earliest and most important creeds was relayed by Paul in his first letter to the Corinthian church, which was written about AD 55.[10]

"It says: 'For I delivered to you as of first importance what I also received, that Christ died for our sins according to the Scriptures, and that he was buried, and that he was raised on the third day according to the Scriptures, and that he appeared to Cephas [Peter], then to the twelve. After that, he appeared to more than five hundred of the brothers at the same time, most of whom are still living, though some have fallen asleep. Then he appeared to James, then to all the apostles . . . .' [1 Corinthians 15:3–7].

"Many scholars believe Paul received this creed from Peter and James while visiting with them in Jerusalem three years after his conversion. That would be within five years of the crucifixion."

Licona's eyes got wide. "Think about that! It's really amazing!" he declared, his voice rising in genuine astonishment. "As one expert said, 'This is the sort of data that historians of antiquity drool over.'[11] Not only is [this declaration about Jesus] extremely early, but it was apparently given to Paul by eyewitnesses or others he deemed reliable, which heightens its credibility even more.

"In fact, this creed has been one of the most formidable obstacles to critics who try to shoot down the resurrection. It's simply gold for a historian.

"Finally, we have written sources, such as Matthew, Mark, Luke, and John. It's widely accepted, even among skeptical historians, that the Gospels were written in the first century. Even very liberal scholars will concede that we have four biographies written within seventy years of Jesus' life that unambiguously report the disciples' claims that Jesus rose from the dead.

"I think an excellent case can be made for dating the Gospels earlier, but let's go with the more generous estimations. That's still extremely close to the events themselves, especially compared to many other ancient historical writings. Our two best sources on Alexander the Great, for instance, weren't written until at least four hundred years after his life.

"So it's really remarkable that in the case of Jesus, we have four biographies that even liberals agree were written within thirty-five to sixty-five years after his execution.

"Then we have the writings of the apostolic fathers, who were said to have known the apostles or were close to others who did. There's a strong likelihood that their writings reflect the teachings of the apostles themselves— and what do they say? That the apostles were dramatically impacted by Jesus' resurrection.

"So think about the depth of evidence we have in these

[Hope is] the unswerving

belief that better days are

ahead, probably in this world

and most certainly in the next.

three categories: Paul, oral tradition, and written reports. In all, we've got nine sources that reflect multiple, very early, and eyewitness testimonies to the disciples' claims that they had seen the risen Jesus. This is something the disciples believed to the core of their being."

"How do you know that?"

"Because we have evidence that the disciples had been transformed to the point where they were willing to endure persecution and even martyrdom. We find this in multiple accounts inside and outside the New Testament.

"Just read through Acts and you'll see how the disciples were willing to suffer for their conviction that Jesus rose from the dead. The church fathers Clement, Polycarp, Ignatius, Tertullian, and Origen—they all confirmed [the disciples' willingness to suffer and die for their belief in Jesus' resurrection]."

"But," I objected, "people of other faiths have been willing to die for their beliefs through the ages. So what does the martyrdom of Jesus' disciples really prove?"

"First, it means that they certainly regarded their beliefs to be true," Licona said. "They didn't willfully lie about this. Liars make poor martyrs. Second, the disciples didn't just *believe* Jesus rose from the dead, but they knew for a fact whether he did. They were on the scene and able to ascertain for sure that he had been resurrected. So it was for the *truth* of the resurrection that they were willing to die.

"This is totally different from a modern-day Islamic terrorist or others willing to die for their beliefs. These people can only have faith that their beliefs are true, but they aren't in a position to know for sure. The disciples, on the other hand, knew for a *fact* whether the resurrection had truly occurred, and knowing the *truth*, they were willing to die for their belief.

"And we're not done yet. We have three more minimal facts to consider."

"Go ahead," I said. "What's your third fact?"

FACT #3: Church persecutor, Saul, converted to become Jesus' apostle, Paul.

"We know from multiple sources that Paul—then known as Saul of Tarsus—was an enemy of the church and committed to persecuting the faithful," Licona said. "But Paul himself said that he was converted to a follower of Jesus because he had personally encountered the resurrected Jesus [Acts 9, 22, 26; 1 Corinthians 9:1, 15:8]. So we have Jesus' resurrection attested by friend and foe alike, which is very significant.

"Then we have six ancient sources in addition to Paul—Luke, Clement of Rome, Polycarp, Tertullian, Dionysius of Corinth, and Origen—reporting that Paul was willing to suffer continually and even die for his beliefs. Again, liars make poor martyrs. So we can be confident that Paul not only claimed the risen Jesus appeared to him, but that he really believed it."

FACT #4: Jesus' skeptical half-brother, James, converted to follow Jesus.

"The next minimal fact involves James, the half-brother of Jesus," Licona said.

"Some people might be surprised that Jesus had siblings," I commented.

"Well, the Gospels tell us that Jesus had at least four half-brothers—James, Joseph, Judas, and Simon—as well as half-sisters whose names we don't know [Matthew 12:46–50, 13:55–56; Mark 3:31–35, 6:3; Luke 8:19–21; John 2:12, 7:3, 5, 10; see also Acts 1:13–14; 1 Corinthians 9:5; Galatians 1:19]. The Jewish historian Josephus referred to 'the brother of Jesus who was called the Christ, whose name was James.'"

"Do we know much about James?" I asked.

"In the second century, Hegesippus reported that

James was a pious Jew who strictly abided by the Jewish law. But more significantly for our purposes, we also have good evidence that James was not a follower of Jesus during Jesus' lifetime."

"How do you know?"

"Mark and John both reported that none of Jesus' brothers believed in him [Mark 3:21, 6:3–4; John 7:3–5]. In fact, John's passage is particularly interesting. It suggests that his brothers had heard about his alleged miracles but didn't believe the reports and were, in a sense, daring their brother to perform them in front of crowds. They were sort of taunting him!" [John 7:3–5].

"Why do you consider the skepticism of Jesus' brothers to be authentic?" I asked.

"Because of the principle of embarrassment," Licona replied. "People are not going to invent a story that's going to embarrass or potentially discredit them, and it would be particularly humiliating for a first-century rabbi not to have his own family as his followers."

"Do you have any other evidence for their skepticism?"

"At the crucifixion, to whom did Jesus entrust the care of his mother? Not to one of his half-brothers, who would be the natural choice, but to John, who was a believer. Why on earth would Jesus do that? I think the inference is very strong: if James or any of his brothers had been believers, they would have gotten the nod instead. So it's reasonable to conclude that none of them was a believer, and Jesus was more concerned with his mother being entrusted into the hands of a spiritual brother.

"Then, however, the pivotal moment occurred: the ancient creedal material in 1 Corinthians 15 tells us that the risen Jesus appeared to James. Again, this is an extremely early account that has all the earmarks of reliability. In fact, James may have been involved in passing along this creed to Paul, in which case James would be personally endorsing what the creed reports about Jesus.

"As a result of his encounter with the risen Jesus, James didn't just become a Christian, but he later became leader of the Jerusalem church. We know this from Acts and Galatians [Acts 15:12–21; Galatians 1:19]. Actually, James was so thoroughly convinced of Jesus' Messiahship because of the resurrection that he died a martyr, as both Christian and non-Christian sources attest.[12]

"So here we have another skeptic who was converted because of a personal encounter with the resurrected Lord and who was willing to die for his convictions."

With that, Licona advanced to the last of his minimal facts.

FACT #5: Jesus' tomb was empty.

"The fifth fact—that the tomb of Jesus was empty—is supported by three strands of evidence: the Jerusalem factor, enemy attestation, and the testimony of women."

"The Jerusalem factor?" I asked. "What's that?"

"This refers to the fact that Jesus was publicly executed and buried in Jerusalem, and then his resurrection was proclaimed in the very same city. In fact, several weeks after the crucifixion, Peter declared to a crowd right there in Jerusalem: 'God has raised this Jesus to life, and we are all witnesses of the fact' [Acts 2:32]. Frankly, it would have been impossible for Christianity to get off the ground in Jerusalem if Jesus' body were still in the tomb. The Roman or Jewish authorities could have simply gone over to his tomb and viewed his corpse, and the misunderstanding would have been over.

"Instead, what we do hear is enemy attestation to the empty tomb. In other words, what were the skeptics saying? That the disciples stole the body. This was reported not only by Matthew, but also by Justin Martyr and Tertullian. Here's the thing: Why would you say someone stole the body if it were still in the tomb? This is an implicit admission that the tomb was empty.

*It would have been impossible
to get Christianity off the
ground in Jerusalem if Jesus'
body were still in the tomb.*

"And enemy attestation is strong evidence in the eyes of historians," I commented.

"That's correct. Here, you've got Jesus' opponents conceding his tomb was vacant. There's no way they would have admitted this if it weren't true. On top of that, the idea that the disciples stole the body is a lame explanation. Are we supposed to believe they conspired to steal the body, pulled it off, and then were willing to suffer continually and even die for what they knew was a lie? That's such an absurd idea that scholars universally reject it today.

"In addition, we have the testimony of women that the tomb was empty. Not only were women the first to discover the vacant grave, but they are mentioned in all four Gospels, whereas male witnesses appear only later and in two of the accounts."

"Why is this important?"

"Because in both first-century Jewish and Roman cultures, women were lowly esteemed and their testimony was considered very questionable. They were certainly considered less credible than men.

"My point is this: If you were going to concoct a story in an effort to fool others, you would never in that day have hurt your own credibility by saying that women discovered the empty tomb. It would be extremely unlikely that the Gospel writers would invent testimony like this, because they wouldn't get any mileage out of it. In fact, it could hurt them. If they had felt the freedom simply to make things up, surely they'd claim that men—maybe Peter or John or even Joseph of Arimathea—were the first to find the tomb empty."

"So this is another example of the criterion of embarrassment."

"Precisely. The best theory for why the Gospel writers included such an embarrassing detail is because that's what actually happened, and they were committed to recording the events accurately, regardless of the credibility problem their accounts created in that culture.

"So the Jerusalem factor, the enemy attestation, and the testimony of women offer good historical reasons for concluding Jesus' tomb was empty. William Ward of Oxford University put it this way: 'All the strictly historical evidence we have is in favor [of the empty tomb], and those scholars who reject it ought to recognize that they do so on some other ground than that of scientific history.'"[13]

MINIMAL FACTS CASE SUMMARIZED

"Okay," I said. "How would you summarize your case?"

"Let's consider what we have. Shortly after Jesus died by crucifixion, his disciples believed that they saw him risen from the dead. They said he appeared not only to individuals but in several group settings as well. The disciples were so convinced and transformed by the experience that they were willing to suffer and even die for their conviction that they had encountered the risen Jesus.

"Then we have two skeptics who regarded Jesus as a false prophet: Paul, the persecutor of the church, and James, who was Jesus' half-brother. They changed their opinions one hundred-and-eighty degrees after encountering the risen Jesus. Like the disciples, they were willing to endure hardship, persecution, and even death rather than disavow their testimony that Jesus' resurrection occurred.

"Thus we have compelling testimony about the resurrection from friends of Jesus, an enemy of Christianity, and a skeptic. Finally, we have strong historical evidence that Jesus' tomb was empty. In fact, even enemies of Christianity admitted it was vacant. Where did the body go? If you asked the disciples, they'd tell you they personally saw Jesus after he returned to life.

"We have to ask ourselves, *What's the best explanation for the evidence, the explanation that doesn't leave out any of the facts or strains to make anything fit?* My conclusion, based on the evidence, is that Jesus did return from the dead."

The Rest of the Story

Licona could have presented all kinds of other historical evidence for the resurrection, but instead he limited himself to five facts that are extremely well-attested historically and that the vast majority of scholars—including skeptics—concede are trustworthy. And these facts are just a skeleton of a much more robust case that could have been made for Jesus' resurrection by using the broader Gospel accounts.[14]

"The rational man," concluded William Lane Craig, "can hardly now be blamed if he infers that at the tomb of Jesus on that early Easter morning a divine miracle has occurred."[15]

But what does all this information mean, and how do arguments that support Jesus' resurrection undergird the case for hope? Here are some key implications of the historical truth of the resurrection of Jesus:

- *Hope in Jesus' wisdom:* If Jesus really is the Son of God, his teachings are more than just good ideas from a wise teacher; they are divine insights on which I can confidently build my life.
- *Hope in Jesus' purity:* If Jesus sets the standard for morality, I can now have an unwavering foundation for my choices and decisions rather than basing them on the ever-shifting sands of expediency and self-centeredness.
- *Hope in Jesus' friendship:* If Jesus really rose from the dead, he's still alive today and I can know him personally.
- *Hope in Jesus' guidance:* If Jesus has divine power, he has the supernatural ability to lead me, help me, and transform me as I follow him.
- *Hope in Jesus' comfort:* If Jesus personally knows the pain of loss and suffering, he can uplift and encourage me in the midst of the turbulence that he himself warned is inevitable in a world corrupted by sin.
- *Hope in Jesus' compassion:* If Jesus loves me as he

says he does, he has my best interests at heart. That means I have nothing to lose and everything to gain by committing myself to him and his purposes.

- *Hope in Jesus' sovereignty:* If Jesus is who he claims to be—God in human flesh—then as my Creator, he rightfully deserves my allegiance, obedience, and worship.
- *Hope in my future with Jesus:* If Jesus conquered death, he can open the door of eternal life for me too.

These arguments convinced me. If Jesus really rose from the dead—which the evidence clearly affirmed—that truth changed everything. After I spent two years investigating the evidence as a skeptic, I had found my Source of hope. That's why I received Jesus' forgiveness and leadership for my life. It was then that I began to live a life of faith, knowing that God had given me "hope and a future" in him (Jeremiah 29:11).[16]

The apostle Peter concluded, "Praise be to the God and Father of our Lord Jesus Christ! In his great mercy he has given us new birth into a living hope through the resurrection of Jesus Christ from the dead, and into an inheritance that can never perish, spoil or fade. This inheritance is kept in heaven for you" (1 Peter 1:3–4).

Chuck Colson, the man who had asked, "Where is the hope?" summed up his thoughts on the matter by saying this: "Our hope is in the power of God working through the hearts of people. That's where our hope lies in this country. And that's where our hope lies in our life."

My friend and former colleague Rick Warren, the pastor of Saddleback Church and the author of *The Purpose Driven Life*,[17] together with his wife, Kay, went through a devastating loss when their twenty-seven-year-old son Matthew took his own life after battling depression and mental illness for years.

About a year after this tragedy, Rick said, "I've often been asked, 'How have you made it? How have you kept going in your pain?' And I've often replied, 'The answer is Easter.'

"You see, the death and the burial and the resurrection of Jesus happened over three days. Friday was the day of suffering and pain and agony. Saturday was the day of doubt and confusion and misery. But *Easter*—that Sunday—was the day of hope and joy and victory.

"And here's the fact of life: you will face these three days over and over and over in your lifetime. And when you do, you'll find yourself asking—as I did—three fundamental questions. Number one, 'What do I do in my days of pain?' Two, 'How do I get through my days of doubt and confusion?' Three, 'How do I get to the days of joy and victory?'

"The answer is Easter. *The answer . . . is Easter.*"[18]

CHAPTER THREE

Hope of a Transformed Life

If anyone is in Christ, the new creation has come:
The old has gone, the new is here! All this is from God,
who reconciled us to himself through Christ.

2 CORINTHIANS 5:17–18

"PEOPLE NEVER CHANGE. THEY JUST BECOME MORE OF who they really are."

That isn't just an Internet meme. It's a cultural cliché that many people accept as established fact: Liars will always lie; cheaters will always cheat; self-centered individuals will never stop looking out for number one.

But if you buy into this thinking—if you accept the idea that people never change and therefore you'll never change—then you're embracing a surefire formula for utter hopelessness about your future.

What's the point in even trying to change? It's all

futile. At best, your efforts will get your hopes up only to have them dashed. Why hold out hope for what's not even possible?

But what does God's Word say? Does it accept the fatalistic determinism embraced by so much of our culture? Thankfully, no. Here's what Paul said in Romans 6:17, 22: "Thanks be to God that, though you used to be slaves to sin, you have come to obey from your heart the pattern of teaching that has now claimed your allegiance. . . . Now that you have been set free from sin and have become slaves of God, the benefit you reap leads to holiness, and the result is eternal life."

Yes, God is still in the business of transforming lives, and that fact ought to give you hope for what he can do in your life as well.

Perhaps some real-life examples of transformed lives would help. Let's examine the stories of two seemingly hopeless individuals, two unlikely candidates for God's grace, who nonetheless found hope through Christ.

THE GODLESS GANG MEMBER

The first story is about a guy named Ronnie Bronski, and it illustrates how Jesus can change a rebellious heart into a reconciled heart. You see, Ronnie was always in trouble. In fact, he was first taken before a judge when he was only eight years old: he had thrown a hammer at someone's head.

As a teenager, Ronnie dropped out of school and joined the Belaires street gang that terrorized parts of Chicago. Ronnie was in and out of juvenile homes and jails. He spent his time hustling for drugs and battling other street gangs that dared venture into Belaires territory.

"Ronnie Bronski was a dangerous kid," said a Chicago police officer. "He liked to fight. His gang was into burglaries, street robberies, and dope. He lived in the streets. The guy was worthless."

When he was twenty-one years old, Ronnie got into big-time trouble. There was a guy named Bob, whose gang from Palmer Street was a rival to the Belaires. One day Bob and his gang jumped one of Ronnie's friends and beat him up. Vowing to avenge the attack, Ronnie borrowed a gun, went into Palmer Street territory, and started hunting for Bob. Soon he saw about half a dozen of the gang members coming out of a tavern. He didn't see Bob, but he saw Bob's brother, Gary. Ronnie figured, "I'll kill Gary, and then when Bob comes to Gary's funeral, I'll ambush and kill him, too. That way I'll get two of them."

So Ronnie Bronski ran up to these gang members and shouted, "Belaires!" That's what they did in street gangs: before shooting somebody, they'd shout the name of their gang. Then Ronnie shoved his gun in Gary's chest and pulled the trigger.

Click.

The gun misfired. Now Ronnie had a half dozen extremely angry gang members standing in front of him. He quickly stepped back, pointed the gun in the air, and pulled the trigger again. This time the gun fired.

The rival gang scattered. Gary ran down the sidewalk with Ronnie chasing after him. As Gary was running, Ronnie was shooting at him, shot after shot. They rounded a corner, and Ronnie was still shooting. Finally, one of the bullets hit Gary in the back, and he fell to the sidewalk. Ronnie caught up to him, turned him over, and aimed the gun right at his face.

Gary begged for his life: "Don't shoot me, man. Don't shoot me again. Don't kill me." Without a twinge of conscience, Ronnie pulled the trigger on the gun one more time.

Click.

The gun was empty. Then Ronnie heard a siren and

God is still in the business

of transforming lives, and

that fact ought to give

you hope for what he can

do in your life as well.

knew the police were coming, so he hid the gun and ran home.

It didn't take much detective work for the police to figure out it was Ronnie Bronski who shot Gary. They issued a warrant for his arrest on a charge of attempted murder.

Ronnie knew that with his criminal record he would get twenty years in prison, and he couldn't stomach that. He decided to flee and live the rest of his life in hiding. So with two hundred dollars in his pocket and his girlfriend at his side, Ronnie got on a bus and headed to Canada. They eventually ended up in Portland, Oregon.

That's where Ronnie got the first job he'd ever had; he was hired as a die cutter in a metal shop. As it turned out, some of the guys working there were Christians whose lives had been transformed by Jesus, and they began talking to Ronnie about God. Ronnie listened and learned, finally coming to understand that nobody is beyond the love of Jesus. Not even a hardcore gang member who had tried to murder somebody in cold blood. After hearing the message and seeing it lived out by his new friends, Ronnie put his full trust in God and became a devoted follower of Christ.

Remember how the Chicago cop had said of Ronnie,

"The guy is worthless"? Here's how a minister in Portland described him after Jesus was in his life: "Ronnie Bronski is one of the most beautiful, loving people I know. He goes out of his way to help people. He is a man of God, and he is very enthusiastic about bringing more people to the Lord."

This former gang member, whose life had been consumed by violence, drugs, and booze, was now giving himself in service to other people. He would go to hospitals to visit the sick and pray with them, and he would go on the streets because kids could relate to him. He would tell them, "You don't have to live this way. There is an alternative through Jesus Christ."

Ronnie married his girlfriend, Debbie, who had also become a Christian, and they had a little girl named Olivia. For the first time in his life, Ronnie was feeling fulfilled and hopeful . . . . But then he began to sense that something was hindering him from growing further. He had been reconciled with God, but he had not been reconciled with society.

He increasingly felt a desire to make things right in his life. He knew this would mean going back to Chicago and facing the felony charge that was pending against him. If he didn't, he would never have real peace.

So two years after he committed the crime, Ronnie saved up enough money to take the train back to Chicago with his wife and eight-month-old daughter. He turned himself in on the charge that could bring him twenty years in the penitentiary.

His lawyer told him, "Ronnie, I think I can get you off of this charge. If you plead 'not guilty,' I don't think the cops will be able to convict you because it's two years old. The witnesses are scattered."

Ronnie said, "It would be a lie for me to come to court and say I'm not guilty. I can't do that."

So Ronnie Bronski walked into Branch 44 of felony court and pleaded guilty. The people in the courtroom were astonished. "The cops weren't out looking for you," they said. "Why didn't you just stay in Portland and keep a low profile? They wouldn't have found you. What made you do this? It doesn't make sense."

Ronnie could only quote 2 Corinthians 5:17: "If anyone is in Christ, the new creation has come: The old has gone, the new is here!" Ronnie even tracked down the guy he had shot and apologized to him.

Through Ronnie Bronski's example, God shows that he can turn real rebels into sanctified followers of Christ, and that ought to give hope to the rest of us.

THE HARD-HEARTED REPORTER

The second story is about how God turned a granite heart into a grateful heart. It's about a reporter who had only one god in his life, and that was his career. He worked for a newspaper in Chicago, and he was given the assignment of moving his office to the West Side to cover the Criminal Courts Building and the Cook County Jail.

Once there, he immersed himself in this sordid subculture, a world of crime and violence where people routinely testified about being defrauded, attacked, robbed, tortured, raped, mutilated, or burned out of their homes.

He would cover these cases, and he would see how the lives of the victims and their families were torn apart. Then he would see the callous defendants, many of whom just didn't seem to care. Over time he became desensitized, and his heart gradually grew hard, like granite.

One October day when this reporter was standing outside the felony court, he met a former fugitive named Ronnie Bronski, who had come all the way back from Portland to turn himself in on a charge that could bring him twenty years in prison.

The reporter grew curious and asked Ronnie to tell

him his story. Ronnie told him about all the crimes and drugs he'd been involved in, but the reporter had heard it all before. Then Ronnie talked about Jesus, and the reporter began to smell a story.

When Ronnie started describing the new life, the purpose, and the hope he had found, the reporter began taking notes. Then the reporter called some of his friends who were gang crime cops in the city, and said, "You know this guy Ronnie Bronski?" They said, "Yeah, we know him. Major gangbanger in Chicago."

The reporter asked, "What's the latest?"

They said, "Well, he was in town, and he came by and talked to us. And you know what? He's a different guy." These hardened cops said, "We believe he is sincere. He has changed. He is a new man."

As a result, this reporter wrote a favorable story about Ronnie. It appeared on page 3 of the Sunday paper with the headline "Reformed Hood Comes Back to Pay His Dues."

The very next day Ronnie appeared in court to be sentenced. His lawyer said to the judge, "I know it's unusual, but could we enter this newspaper article as evidence?" The judge agreed, took the article, and read it. He looked at the other facts of the case and read the sworn statements from Ronnie's Christian friends in Portland, who said that he was a changed man.

Finally, the judge looked over the bench at Ronnie. "I could send you to the pen," he said. "I *ought* to send you to the pen for what you have done."

Then he added, "But I don't think you are a threat to society anymore. I think it's true that you are a new man. So I'm not going to send you to the pen. I am going to put you on probation. Ronnie, go home to your family."

Ronnie was stunned. He thought he was going to get hammered by the judge, but instead he was walking out a free man.

Outside the court the incredulous reporter went up to him and asked, "Ronnie, what is your reaction to this?"

Said Ronnie: "The judge just showed me grace, sort of like Jesus Christ did . . . . Jesus Christ can show you grace too."

The reporter's reaction? He said to himself, *I am sure Ronnie Bronski is a changed man, but it was probably just a positive mental attitude that did it. There is no God, so "God" didn't do this. Ronnie turned himself around. And it's a great story.*

But a seed had been planted in the rocky soil of that reporter's heart, and time after time he would think back

Once your heart has been seized by God's grace, once you're astonished to your core by the fact that the Creator of the universe wants to forgive your sins and spend eternity with you, then you'll never want to lose the wonder of God's undeserved and unending love.

to the story he had written about Ronnie. He would ask himself, *What was it that really changed him?*

About four years after that encounter, the reporter's wife put her faith in Christ. He began to see changes in her. These very subtle but very attractive changes were like a blossoming of her personality.

His wife and her friends started praying for this hard-hearted reporter, focusing on Ezekiel 36:26 (NASB). It says, "I will give you a new heart and put a new spirit within you; and I will remove the heart of stone . . . and give you a heart of flesh." And that's exactly what God ended up doing in his life.

I should know. *I was that reporter.*

I wrote the story about Ronnie Bronski that appeared in the *Chicago Tribune*. And some time later, after spending nearly two years investigating the claims of Christianity, I became convinced that there is a God and that I could be reconciled with him through Jesus Christ. I also realized that Ronnie Bronski isn't a new man because of a positive mental attitude, but because Jesus turned his heart inside out. And I opened up my heart to Christ.

I don't have a violent past or police record like Ronnie, but I had a heart that was full of deceit, pride, and evil. Before God, I was just as guilty as Ronnie, and because of

Jesus I am now just as forgiven as Ronnie is. God answered my wife's and her friends' prayers: he transformed my granite heart into a grateful heart.

Oh, and Ronnie? He's a pastor now in Vancouver, Washington—at a church that is aptly named "Song of Hope."

SINGING OF HOPE

When Leslie and I got married, we weren't following Jesus. Because her mother was from Scotland, the two of them thought it would be great to have a bagpiper at our wedding reception since that's such a central part of Scottish culture. As Leslie and I walked arm-in-arm into the banquet, I caught the melody of a song being played. I remember saying to myself, *What a catchy tune.*

Later I found out its name: "Amazing Grace." I didn't know anything about the song then or, for that matter, anything about the concept of grace. But ever since Jesus revolutionized my heart, I can't sing "Amazing Grace" without tears in my eyes. In fact, I was at church one night during a Communion service when we sang the song.

I was crying so hard that it was embarrassing. I went around behind the bleachers where I was sitting so nobody would see me, and I bawled. I said, "God, I just pray that I will never again, ever in my life, be able to sing 'Amazing Grace' without feeling it. I always want to feel it. Until the day I die, I always want to have tears in my eyes when I sing that song. Never, ever let me become immune to the wonder of your grace."

Sometimes we need to pause and reflect on how incredible it is that Jesus offers forgiveness, cleansing, and hope to rebellious people like Ronnie Bronski, to hard-hearted people like me, and to people like you.

Once your heart has been seized by God's grace, once you're astonished to your core by the fact that the Creator of the universe wants to forgive your sins and spend eternity with you, then you'll never want to lose the wonder of God's undeserved and unending love.

So do whatever it takes to keep the wonder of God's grace fresh in your heart. Use the simple, age-old practices of daily times of prayer, Scripture reading, worship, and fellowship to make sure you stay attuned to the hope God has given you.

Or if you have never experienced that grace, then do what Ronnie did. Go, in effect, into court before God and plead guilty. You may be afraid you'll get hammered by the Judge, but humbly admit, "I've broken your laws, and

I know I deserve to pay the penalty. But, God, I am sorry. I want to make things right. And I want to be reconciled to you."

When you do that, you are going to get mercy that exceeds even what Ronnie Bronski got in Branch 44. God is going to look at you and say, "My Son has already paid your penalty. He did it when he died on the cross. He has served your sentence. He has paid for every evil thought you've ever had and every wrong you've ever done. Forget probation. I am going to set you free from guilt and punishment. More than that, I'm adopting you into my family, now and for all of eternity."

That is amazing grace. That is the kind of grace that transforms us and gives us *real* hope.

> *Amazing grace! How sweet the sound*
> *That saved a wretch like me.*
> *I once was lost, but now am found,*
> *Was blind, but now I see.*
>
> *'Twas grace that taught my heart to fear,*
> *And grace my fears relieved.*
> *How precious did that grace appear*
> *The hour I first believed.*

Through many dangers, toils, and snares
*   I have already come;*
'Tis grace hath brought me safe thus far
*   And grace will lead me home.*

The Lord has promised good to me
*   His word my* **hope** *secures;*
He will my shield and portion be,
*   As long as life endures.*

Yea, when this flesh and heart shall fail,
*   and mortal life shall cease,*
I shall possess within the veil,
*   A life of joy and peace.*

When we've been there ten thousand years
*   Bright shining as the sun,*
We've no less days to sing God's praise
*   Than when we've first begun.*[1]

CHAPTER FOUR

Hope for Today . . . and Tomorrow

Hope does not disappoint us, because God has poured out his love into our hearts by the Holy Spirit, whom he has given us.
ROMANS 5:5

OUR GOD IS THE *GOD OF HOPE*, THE *GOD OF THE SECOND chance*, and the *God who transforms* the lives of seemingly hopeless people, including characters like former gang member Ronnie Bronski and a hard-hearted reporter.

And like *you* too.

But it's often easier to count on God to redeem our past than it is to trust him with our present and our future. Our tendency is to begin our spiritual journeys with a childlike belief in God's miraculous power, and then gradually revert to a reliance on our own human efforts. It was because of this tendency that the apostle Paul challenged the believers in Galatia: "Are you so foolish? After beginning by means of the Spirit, are you now trying to finish by means of the flesh?" (Galatians 3:3).

The all-too-frequent answer then—as now—was a resounding *yes.*

I don't mean to sound like a conspiracy theorist, but I think there's a diabolical plot afoot, one designed to tell us that it might make sense to trust God with our problems of yesterday, but not for those of today or tomorrow.

"Sure," Satan whispers, "the Big Guy reached down and helped you turn things around after what was a pretty sordid past. But he has a whole world to look after, with countless emergencies happening all the time. So don't expect *him* to be intervening from this point forward in your insignificant life. You've already gotten all the help you're going to get. From here on out, you're on your own!"

This enemy of our souls, the one the Bible calls "the accuser" (Revelation 12:10), does all he can to drain us of hope. Were it not for God's ongoing infusions of power in our lives, we'd be in real trouble.

Thankfully, God is not just all-powerful; he is also *a power-sharing God.* He cares so much about us that he's willing to imbue us with some of his strength *if* we choose to tap into it. Put another way, God can give us power as power is needed.

A PSALM OF POWER

Let me illustrate this with a passage of Scripture that is not only magnificent in its descriptive force, but it also contains an encouraging surprise ending.

Trying to creatively express the extent of God's incredible strength, King David harkened back to his days as a shepherd when he would watch awesome thunderstorms rumble through the desert with frightening intensity. Based on these experiences David extolled God's great power in Psalm 29:

> *The voice of the LORD is over the waters. (v. 3)*

Apparently, this storm was roaring in from the Mediterranean.

> *The God of glory thunders,*
> *   the LORD thunders over the mighty waters.*
> *The voice of the LORD is powerful;*
> *   the voice of the LORD is majestic.*

> *The voice of the LORD breaks the cedars;*
> *the LORD breaks in pieces the cedars of*
> *Lebanon. (vv. 3–5)*

Do you know how big the cedars get in Lebanon? They can grow up to thirty feet in diameter and rise as high as a twelve-story building. But David was saying that a mere whisper from God is enough to instantaneously splinter those towering trees into kindling. That's power!

> *[God] makes Lebanon leap like a calf,*
> *Sirion like a young wild ox. (v. 6)*

Sirion is a nine-thousand-foot mountain. In other words, God's voice is like a mighty earthquake that makes the plains and mountain ranges shake and quiver and undulate and dance.

> *The voice of the LORD strikes*
> *with flashes of lightning. (v. 7)*

Think about the incredible power released by the one hundred lighting strikes happening around the planet *every second*. Each lightning flash discharges up to one hundred million volts of electricity and can raise the temperature of the air 50,000 degrees Fahrenheit, which is five times hotter than the surface of the sun![1] Yet a single utterance from the lips of the Lord is far more potent than all of the lightning in the two thousand thunderstorms taking place around the world at any given moment.[2]

> *The voice of the LORD shakes the desert;*
> *the LORD shakes the Desert of Kadesh. (v. 8)*

Kadesh is in the south; Sirion is in the north. These references tell us that God's tremendous power is manifest across the entire land. Nobody can flee from it.

> *The voice of the LORD twists the oaks*
> *and strips the forests bare. (v. 9)*

You may remember the photographs after Mount St. Helens erupted in the state of Washington in 1980. In a blast that had the explosive force of five hundred atomic bombs, giant trees over an area of 230 square miles were toppled like matchsticks and stripped clean of their bark. Millions and millions of trees were destroyed, enough to construct three hundred thousand houses. Yet that is all child's play for the God of the universe. It would only take a murmur from him to flatten the entire 815 million acres of the Amazon rainforest.

So what should be our response to our God whose strength is so immense that it completely dwarfs the incredible energy released in an epic desert thunderstorm? David's response serves as a great example:

> *And in his temple all cry, "Glory!"*
> *The Lord sits enthroned over the flood;*
> *the Lord is enthroned as King forever. (vv. 9–10)*

What other reaction can we have but to worship such a mighty and breathtakingly awesome God who rightfully reigns over all of his creation?

Then, suddenly, David's poem takes a surprising turn. After describing God's incredible power, the psalm concludes suddenly and with a totally unexpected twist:

> *The Lord gives strength to his people;*
> *the Lord blesses his people with peace. (v. 11)*

Here's the point: our omnipotent God doesn't hoard his power. Instead, he is an empowering Deity who cares deeply

Our omnipotent God doesn't hoard his power. Instead, he is an empowering Deity who cares deeply about the people he created and who wants to share his strength with us.

about the people he created and who wants to share his strength with us. That's really good news, because it means that in him we can find peace when we're panicky, endurance when we're empty, and courage when we're cowardly.

"For God did not give us a spirit of timidity," said the apostle Paul, "but a spirit of power, of love and of self-discipline" (2 Timothy 1:7). What a hope-filled promise from an incredibly mighty God!

Who doesn't need power like that in their daily life? Who wouldn't want to be on the receiving end of God's generous offer to infuse us with his supernatural strength as we face the challenges of today and tomorrow?

But the real question is *how* that happens. Practically speaking, what can we do to benefit from that divine strength?

TAPPING INTO GOD'S POWER

Accessing the power of God isn't a matter of pushing the right buttons or chanting the right words. Instead, there are some specific biblical steps we can take when we're feeling overwhelmed by tragedy, vulnerable to temptation, or too weak to grow more like Christ—or just generally timid, defeated, or bereft of hope.

I call these steps the "Five A's" to make them easier to remember. I discovered them while searching the pages of the Bible. In applying them in my own life through the years, I've invariably found that they are a tremendous help. As you read them, consider how they can help position you to better tap into the power of our omnipotent God.

1st "A": ADMIT That You're Weak Without God.

My first reaction in a crisis is to try to forge through it by myself, because I don't like to depend on anyone else. But here's the thing: *we can't be filled with the power of God until we let go of the false pretense that we can get by on our own.*

We need to admit that we can't get through even the challenges of today—much less the problems that lie ahead—without some outside intervention. So often in Scripture, from Moses to Paul, we see the same pattern: people admitting their weakness first and then God filling them with his power. "Humble yourselves, therefore, under God's mighty hand," Peter admonished, "that he may lift you up in due time" (1 Peter 5:6).

And Paul wrote, "But [the Lord] said to me, 'My grace is sufficient for you, for my power is made perfect in weakness.' Therefore I will boast all the more gladly about my weaknesses, so that Christ's power may rest on me" (2 Corinthians 12:9).

The longer we stubbornly resist the obvious—that we're ultimately powerless by ourselves—the deeper we sink into the mire. After all, we can't reach out and grab on to God's strength if we're clutching the bootstraps of our own self-sufficiency.

"Nothing so furthers our prayer life as the feeling of our own helplessness," Ole Hallesby wrote in his classic book *Prayer.* "It is only when we are helpless that we open our hearts to Jesus, and let him help us in our distress . . . ."[3]

2nd "A": AFFIRM God's Power and Presence.

Once we come face-to-face with the reality of our own weakness, we need to remind ourselves that we follow an all-powerful God who has a consistent track record of infusing his followers with his divine strength.

The Bible says we need to keep that truth at the forefront of our minds: "Look to the LORD and his strength; seek his face always. Remember the wonders he has done, his miracles and the judgments he pronounced" (1 Chronicles 16:11–12).

In other words, let yourself dwell on how God empowered Moses, strengthened David, rescued Daniel, emboldened Esther, restored Peter, and energized Paul. Remember that, time after time, God has proven himself trustworthy.

You can do this by regularly immersing yourself in these and similar stories in God's Word. The real-world accounts of God's intervention in the lives of ordinary men and women will increase your sense of hope in his abiding presence and power. As Paul puts it, "Faith comes by hearing, and hearing by the word of God" (Romans 10:17 NKJV).

In addition to acknowledging God's power, we also should affirm his desire to be present in our lives.

Years ago our daughter Alison was in a high school choir that sang "From a Distance" by Julie Gold. When they came to the lyrics "God is watching us from a distance," I wanted to stand up and shout, "Hey, that's not true!"

For Alison's sake I didn't do it (for that she was very grateful), but the truth is that God doesn't just see us from afar. He's here. He's close. He's accessible. Theologically, we know that God is *transcendent* (above all) and *immanent* (close to us and involved in our lives). The Lord told Joshua, for example, to "be strong and courageous. Do not be afraid; do not be discouraged, for *the* LORD *your God will be with you wherever you go*" (Joshua 1:9).

Our confidence, strength, and overall sense of hope in the midst of life's challenges are bolstered when we remember that the God who empowered his people throughout the ages is the very same God who wants to be present in our life today as well as tomorrow.

3rd "A": ALIGN Yourself with God's Will.

There was once a country-western song on the radio that kept repeating the refrain "Looking for love in all the wrong places." Well, in a similar vein, we're often looking for God's strength, but for all the wrong reasons. But God's power isn't accessed through some kind of spiritual wall socket that we can plug into for just anything we might want.

Jesus said, "I am the vine; you are the branches" (John 15:5). That means you and I need to be intimately connected with God and his purposes. He went on to say in that same verse, "If you remain in me and I in you, you will bear much fruit." In other words, when we're living in harmony with God, he's willing to give us his power to accomplish great things.

The verse concludes with this stark but important reminder: "Apart from me you can do nothing." When we're independently pursuing our own agenda, we shouldn't expect that God will want to contribute to it.

Think about it. It wouldn't make sense for God to supernaturally renew our strength so we could pursue a pet project that runs contrary to his best plans for our life. We need to make sure we're traveling the road he has laid out for us before we seek his help in moving ahead. Looking at it another way, if we know that he wants what's best for us, wouldn't it make sense for us to get in sync with his plan?

Aligning ourselves with God's will begins when we initially put our trust in Jesus as the Forgiver of our sins and the Leader of our life. Then we can start to discern more and more of his specific guidance as we grow in our relationship with him and increasingly submit to his agenda for our lives.

As we mature in our faith, we become more and more adept at understanding God's will. We grow familiar with his voice. We immerse ourselves in his Book and consistently test every thought, idea, and action against its teachings. We receive guidance from his indwelling Holy Spirit. We seek wise counsel from other Christians. We develop confidence that we are heading in God's direction, that we're going the right way. And he'll be available to encourage and empower us along the journey.

4th "A": ASK God for the Power You Need.

When I was in high school, my older brother, Ray, bought a shiny new convertible Corvette. It was gorgeous. Of course I wanted to borrow it, but I was too intimidated to come right out and ask him. So I would beat around the bush, although not in a very subtle way.

"I guess the car's just going to sit there all night, huh?" I'd say casually. "All alone. All by itself . . . Sort of a shame. It looks like it might need some exercise."

I'd go on and on until Ray would finally exclaim, "Look, Lee, if you want to borrow the car, just *ask*!" Amazingly, when I finally voiced a real request, he actually let me take his Corvette out for a cruise!

Similarly, we often want desperately for God to intervene in our lives, but we beat around the bush. We don't just come out and ask him to act on our behalf. Yet the Bible tells us forthrightly that "you do not have because you do not ask God" (James 4:2). God himself is saying that we need to just come right out and tell him the desires of our heart!

Having admitted our inability to handle the matter

ourselves, having affirmed God's power and presence in our lives, and having aligned ourselves with God and his purposes, we should forthrightly and specifically ask him for his supernatural help.

Sometimes I've done that and—*wow!*—experienced a flood of boldness, courage, and effectiveness that I can only attribute to the work of God in my life. And talk about a renewal of *hope!* That moment completely changes my perspective about my current challenges as well as the problems I know I'll face in the future.

But I'll be honest. I don't always end up feeling that way. There have been times when I've gone through those first four steps, but I didn't feel any different. I was still scared and weak. Has that ever happened to you? If so, what should you do? I've found that the best strategy is to move on to the final step.

5th "A": ACT in Obedience to God.
My former colleague Bill Hybels once pointed out this scriptural pattern: even when we don't feel empowered, if we nevertheless take action by obediently proceeding down the road God wants us to walk, then he will give us power as power is needed. Or, as Bill put it, God will give us *power along the way.*

With faith—with a hope-
filled trust that God will
come through for us—plus
obedient action, we'll receive
power as power is needed.

As an example, Bill pointed to a story in Luke 17, where ten lepers called out to Jesus from a distance, asking him to heal them. Jesus responded by simply telling them to "go show yourselves to the priests" to confirm they'd been healed. But at that moment they still had leprosy, so this must have been confusing to them. Still, by faith, they followed Jesus' instructions and headed down the road to talk to the priests. Luke 17:14 tells us that "as they went"—as they moved forward in obedience—"they were cleansed." God healed them along the way.

Hybels also said to think of Jesus in the Garden of Gethsemane. Jesus was overwhelmed with emotion over his impending death. He felt weak and fearful, but after praying and confirming that he was aligned with his Father's will, he obediently walked out of that garden, into the hands of his betrayer, and down the path toward his sacrificial death. And the Father gave him strength as strength was needed.

Jesus was therefore able to endure the whipping, the beating, the mocking, the crown of thorns, the searing nails in his hands and feet, and the crushing weight of the world's sins that was placed upon his shoulders. He got through all of it until finally declaring, "It is finished"

(John 19:30). Jesus had paid the price once and for all to redeem the world.

But don't miss this point: God the Father made sure his Son had the strength he needed as he carried out his all-important mission of redemption.

And when you and I walk down the road of obedience to God, even when we're not feeling empowered, what we're doing is demonstrating faith. Faith isn't merely believing something; faith is belief *plus* behavior. It's believing something and taking action in accordance with what we believe. Someone once defined faith as "belief gone courageous."

The Bible says, "Without faith it is impossible to please God" (Hebrews 11:6). But Scripture also teaches that *with* faith—with a hope-filled trust that God will come through for us—plus obedient action, we'll receive power as power is needed.

THE "FIVE A'S" IN ACTION

I've seen God's power demonstrated in my own life time after time. For example, a number of years ago, I knew I needed to reconcile with someone I had mistreated, but I felt too intimidated and embarrassed to do it. I knew it would be hard for me to admit my fault. I was afraid he might react with rage because of how I'd hurt him. And I wasn't even sure how I would bring up the subject without feeling awkward.

But I remembered the principles we've talked about in this chapter. I admitted to God that I needed his strength. I affirmed that he is powerful and that he was with me. I knew I was aligned with his will, because the Bible tells us, "If it is possible, as far as it depends on you, live at peace with everyone" (Romans 12:18). And I prayed, asking God for the courage to follow through.

Honestly, even after all of that I didn't feel a sudden surge of spiritual power. In fact, I still felt apprehensive and inadequate. Even so, I made the conscious decision to take the fifth step. That meant I had to simply take action and do what I knew God wanted me to do.

I walked over to the phone and forced myself to pick it up and dial the man's number. I chose to trust that if I walked down the road of obedience, God would give me power as power was needed. And sure enough, as the conversation unfolded, God emboldened and strengthened me throughout what was still a difficult talk, but today I'm reconciled with that friend.

So if you need God's power in your life, don't forget

that you must *take action*. Even if you feel overwhelmed by a personal loss or tragedy, or maybe plagued by trepidation about what the future will hold, put one foot in front of the other and trust that God will give you the strength you need.

Brother Andrew can testify to the effectiveness of this action step. He gained the nickname "God's Smuggler" at the height of the Cold War by creatively sneaking millions of Bibles into closed countries. That effort has continued throughout the world, including in societies so hostile to Christianity that no one thought anybody could penetrate them.[4] How was Brother Andrew able to get through?

Once he felt confident that God was leading him to take Christian materials into a nation, Brother Andrew took concrete action, obeying even when the door of entry seemed securely shut. As he drove toward the border with his Bibles, God would always empower him along the way and enable him to fulfill his mission. I love the way Brother Andrew described it:

The door may seem closed, but it's only closed the way a supermarket door is closed. It stays shut when you remain at a distance, but as you deliberately move toward it, a magic eye above it sees you coming, and the door opens. God is waiting for us to walk forward in obedience so he can open the door for us to serve him.[5]

When you demonstrate faith by taking specific steps in obedience to God, he is more than willing to intervene supernaturally in your life. Through it all, just hold on to the words of King David: "Commit your way to the LORD; trust in him *and he will do this*: He will make your righteous reward shine like the dawn, your vindication like the noonday sun" (Psalm 37:5–6).

That promise ought to give you confident hope in God's help and strength through all of the challenges you'll face today, tomorrow, and for the rest of your life. And into eternity as well, but that's the topic of a later chapter.

CHAPTER FIVE

Hope That Transcends Doubt

"Why are you troubled, and why do doubts rise in your minds? Look at my hands and my feet. It is I myself! Touch me and see."

JESUS IN LUKE 24:38–39

IF *ANYBODY* SHOULD HAVE BEEN IMMUNE TO SPIRITUAL doubt, it would be John the Baptist. The Bible says of John: "He came as a witness to testify concerning that light," meaning Jesus, the Light of the World. John did this "so that through him all might believe. He himself was not the light; he came only as a witness to the light" (John 1:7–8).

In fact, John's whole life was about paving the way for Jesus. He confidently pointed to Jesus and declared,

"Look, the Lamb of God, who takes away the sin of the world!" (John 1:29). He baptized Jesus and then witnessed the heavens open up and God proclaim, "You are my Son, whom I love; with you I am well pleased" (Mark 1:11).

John was also the prophet who, in the face of strong opposition from the religious leaders concerning Jesus, defiantly declared, "I have seen and I testify that this is God's Chosen One" (John 1:34). I don't think you could have found a bolder or more powerful witness for Jesus than John the Baptist.

Yet some time later, after John had been arrested by King Herod and was wallowing in prison as he awaited execution, questions began to swirl in John's mind. Suddenly he wasn't so sure about Jesus anymore. Gradually, the prophet who had brought so many people hope was finding himself drained of hope, and he reached out for reassurance.

The Gospel writer Luke described how John sent two of his friends to track down Jesus and ask him point-blank, "Are you the one who is to come, or should we expect someone else?" (Luke 7:20). That was John's way of saying, "I used to be convinced you were the Messiah, but now . . . Well, I'm wondering . . . ."[1]

An Epidemic of Doubt

It would be easy to be critical of John the Baptist *if we weren't so much like him!* How utterly human it is to plummet from the mountaintops of spiritual certainty to the depths of doubt and despair. How normal it is to feel one moment like an invincible carrier of God's hope and the next to feel completely hopeless. We see this happen to many of the Bible's heroes, including Abraham, Moses, King David, Elijah, Peter on the night of Jesus' arrest, and the so-called Doubting Thomas after Jesus rose from the dead.

I know I've gone through bouts of doubt that felt like they could be lethal to my faith. How about you?

Perhaps you've questioned whether God has really forgiven you or whether he can keep forgiving you when, as a Christian, you've failed to do what you knew he was telling you to do. Or you've wondered whether the Bible can be trusted. Or you can't reconcile the world's suffering with a loving God. Or you've read an article by a skeptical scientist or liberal theologian that kicked the legs of your faith right out from under you.

The truth is that a spiritual virus has been going around Christian circles for centuries, and it's called *doubt.* If you haven't caught it yet, you probably will at some point. In fact, I'm convinced that we could divide Christians into three groups. The first would consist of those who have doubted. The second would be those who haven't doubted yet but who will. The third group would be those who have completely shut off their brains!

If you're a thinking person—if you seriously contemplate your faith and what it means to follow Jesus—then chances are that every once in a while you're going to come down with the virus and have some troubling questions, issues, concerns, uncertainties, or hesitations.

By the way, this is not just a Christian phenomenon. As a former atheist, I can personally testify that atheists also doubt their position from time to time. C. S. Lewis wrote, "Now that I am a Christian I do have moods in which the whole thing looks very improbable; but when I was an atheist I had moods in which Christianity looked terribly probable."[2] Even the most doubtful of doubters will sometimes doubt their own doubts!

So the issue isn't whether you will catch the doubt virus; we're all infected to some degree. The real question is this: *How can we prevent that virus from turning into a virulent disease that ultimately ravages our faith?* Or perhaps this is a better question: *How can we respond to our doubts in ways that will help us emerge even stronger as a result?* As incredible as it sounds, a bout of doubt may turn out to be one of the healthiest and most hope-inspiring experiences you'll ever go through.

DOUBTS ABOUT DOUBT

There's no doubt about it: doubt scares many Christians. They stare into the darkness at night, pestered by vague uncertainties and persistent questions that make them feel anxious and vulnerable, almost as if they were experiencing something I call *spiritual vertigo.*

Making matters worse, most Christians are reluctant to breathe a word about this, because they don't want to be embarrassed. "I was so glad to hear you say that doubt is common because I thought I was the only one," a woman told me after I spoke on this topic. "I was afraid to admit I had questions. I didn't want everybody around here to think I was some kind of wimp!"

When we keep our doubts inside, we unwittingly give them more power over us. On the other hand, when we finally let them emerge and we face them squarely, it's amazing how their influence can dissipate.

So let's put the doubt virus under the microscope

where we can expose it to scrutiny and destroy some of our misconceptions that give it undue strength. And believe me! There are plenty of misunderstandings about doubt.

First Misunderstanding: What Doubt Really Is

Many Christians think that doubt is the opposite of faith, but it isn't. The opposite of faith is *unbelief*, and that's an extremely important distinction to understand.

In his book *In Two Minds*, Os Guinness said, "Doubt comes from a word meaning 'two.' To believe is to be 'in one mind' about accepting something as true; to disbelieve is to be 'in one mind' about rejecting it. To doubt is to waver between the two, to believe and disbelieve at once and so to be 'in two minds.'"[3]

Guinness also pointed out that in the Bible, unbelief refers to a willful refusal to believe or a deliberate decision to disobey God. But doubt is different. When we doubt, we're being indecisive or ambivalent about an issue. We haven't come down squarely on the side of disbelief or belief; we're simply stuck over some questions or concerns.

"Doubt does not mean denial or negation," wrote

An authentic relationship
means telling the truth about
how we feel, and that's
the kind of relationship
God wants with us.

Karl Barth. "Doubt only means swaying and staggering between Yes and No."[4]

In his insightful book *If I Really Believe, Why Do I Have These Doubts?* my friend Lynn Anderson candidly described his struggles with faith. He explained that nonbelievers are people "who have made a conscious or unconscious choice not to have faith." In contrast, doubters may be uncertain about whether they have real faith or they may not know exactly what to believe, but "they still want to have faith."[5]

Let me offer some words of encouragement: *You can have a strong faith and still struggle with doubt.* You can be heaven-bound and nevertheless express uncertainty over some theological issues. You can be a full-fledged Christian without absolutely settling every question of life once and for all. In fact, it has been said that struggling with God over the issues of life doesn't show a *lack* of faith; that struggling with God *is* faith. If you don't believe me, just peruse the Old Testament book of Psalms!

"True believers can experience doubt," said Gary Habermas, a biblical scholar who has extensively researched this topic. "In both the Old and New Testaments, believers clearly express wide ranges of questioning, especially on such topics as pain and evil, God's personal dealing with his people, and the issue of evidence for one's belief. On each of those subjects, doubt is clearly expressed by prominent believers."[6]

So go ahead and breathe a sigh of relief. Those words might be just what you needed to hear to begin neutralizing the anxiety that the doubt virus has been generating inside you, robbing you of the hope your Christian faith ought to give you.

SECOND MISUNDERSTANDING: DOUBT IS A SIN TO BE FORGIVEN

Not only is doubt different from disbelief, but contrary to popular opinion, doubt is not a sinful offense. God doesn't condemn us when we ask him questions.

Let's go back to the example of John the Baptist.[7] How did Jesus react to John's questions? Not by slam-dunking John. Not by shaming him. Not by declaring, "How dare he have a hesitation about me!" Instead, Jesus responded with gentleness and provided information he knew would help quell John's doubts. Jesus told John's disciples, "Go back and report to John what you have seen and heard: The blind receive sight, the lame walk, those who have leprosy are cleansed, the deaf hear, the dead are raised, and the good news is proclaimed to the poor. Blessed is anyone who does not stumble on account of me" (Luke 7:22–23).

That is, Jesus instructed John's disciples to provide John with evidence they had seen that confirmed that Jesus was indeed the Messiah. Then, Jesus suggested, John's plague of doubt would be healed and his hope restored.

What's really interesting is how this incident affected Jesus' view of John. People plagued by doubt might assume that John's questions, though answered by Jesus, would have disqualified him from any significant role in God's kingdom. But instead Jesus declared, "I tell you, among those born of women there is no one greater than John" (Luke 7:28).

Think about that. Jesus uttered those words about John the Doubter, and he did so right after addressing John's worst recorded bout with doubt! So in the midst of your own sincere questions and concerns, while you're wrestling with your own honest uncertainties, you can rest assured that Jesus won't slam-dunk you either.

Don't you think God would rather have you be honest with him about your doubts than have you profess a phony faith? He knows what's going on inside us anyway;

it's absurd to think we can mask our doubts from him. An authentic relationship means telling the truth about how we feel, and that's the kind of relationship God wants with us.

THIRD MISUNDERSTANDING:
DOUBT INEVITABLY DOES DAMAGE

Another common misconception is that the doubt virus is always detrimental to our spiritual health. However, the truth is that God can use our doubts to produce positive side effects.

Using a medical analogy, overcoming a bout of doubt is like getting an immunization. To help your body ward off a disease in the future, doctors inject you with a small amount of the virus that causes that very same illness so you will build up antibodies that will battle off that sickness if it ever threatens you. In the long run your body is actually healthier for the experience.

Similarly, when you're infected with the doubt virus and it compels you to seek answers to your questions, then you will ultimately emerge stronger than ever. Your faith has been confirmed once more. And you end up gaining greater confidence for dealing with doubt in the future.

That's what happened to me when I was a fairly new Christian and volunteered to respond to cards submitted by church attenders who had questions. One Sunday a twelve-year-old girl turned in a card that simply said she wanted to know more about Jesus. "Could you and your wife come have dinner with me and my dad so we could talk?" she asked in a subsequent phone conversation.

"Of course!" I replied. I couldn't imagine a better way to spend an evening than telling a child and her father about Jesus.

But when Leslie and I arrived at their house, I glanced at the coffee table and saw a stack of scholarly books written by critics of Christianity. It turned out that the girl's father was a scientist who had been studying critiques of the faith for a long time.

Over pizza and soft drinks, he peppered me with questions until midnight, and many of his challenges caught me off guard. Frankly, a few sent tremors through my faith.

I finally said, "I can't answer all of your questions, but I don't think that after two thousand years you've come up with an issue that will finally destroy the foundations of Christianity. I'm confident there are good answers to your questions. Let me do some research and get back to you."

This doubt-generating experience prompted me to delve into new areas of research, and I soon found satisfying answers that boosted my confidence in Christianity to even greater heights. In short, my bout with doubt was a spiritual immunization that had a positive impact on me. As a result I'm better equipped today to handle these kinds of questions when they arise.

Author Mark Littleton agrees that this kind of experience can be tremendously beneficial. "Through doubt we can learn more than through naive trust," he said. "Truth can be tested. Doubt is the fire through which it passes. But when it has been tried, it will come forth as gold."[8]

There's another way that doubt can be healthy for us: it can guard us from our own gullibility. Most religious cults, for instance, would go out of business immediately if their members would exercise a healthy dose of doubt about the biblical interpretations, broader teachings, and actual practices of the groups they're part of.

"Test everything," cautioned the apostle Paul. "Hold on to the good" (1 Thessalonians 5:21). When teaching doesn't square with Scripture, it's time to question that teacher and let our doubts lead us away from harm. Godly teachers encourage questions; those who demand unthinking agreement have something to hide.

Faith is the decision to
trust and follow Jesus
Christ, and it need not ebb
and flow based on how
emotionally charged we feel.

The doubt virus, then, can serve us well in certain circumstances if we respond to it appropriately. But despite doubt's potential upside, it's never a good idea to go out of our way to find and foster doubt. Whenever we experience uncertainty we should work expeditiously to resolve our questions and move past them.

Reclaiming Hope

I don't want to suggest that there's some spiritual elixir that will cure you of your doubts. Some people end up living with a frustrating low-grade infection of doubt over long periods. At the same time, though, there is hope.

"When does doubt become unbelief?" asked Alister McGrath. "Answer: when you let it."[9]

So don't let it. By taking action, you can prevent questions, concerns, or doubts from getting out of control and blossoming into full-fledged disbelief.

Through the years I've talked with people who were struggling with doubt, ranging from those who were merely pestered by questions to some who would qualify as "congenital doubters." I've found that there are five steps that can help anyone battle the doubt virus. To make these easy to remember, I've used the acronym FAITH, with each letter signifying one of the five steps.

Step #1: FIND the Root of Your Doubt.

This is the diagnostic phase, the time when you delve into what's behind your particular strain of doubt. Is the root *intellectual*, caused by questions in your mind? Or is it *emotional*, based on feelings or lack of feelings? Or is it *volitional*, stemming from your will and the choices you make that hamper your relationship with God?

If the root of our doubt is intellectual, we might start to wonder whether it is rational to believe in angels, demons, heaven, hell, miracles, and the resurrection. There is good evidence to support these beliefs, but we become vulnerable to the doubt virus if we don't know *why* we believe what we believe.

Doubt can also result from not knowing *what* you should believe. Having a distorted or imbalanced view of God can set you up for unwarranted disappointment in him. For example, if you think God has promised to answer every single one of your prayers the way you want him to, you're going to develop doubts when he doesn't seem to come through for you.

Or is the problem emotional? For some people, faith is

built entirely on feelings. They had a euphoric experience when they gave their life to Christ and were emotionally pumped up for a while. Eventually that spiritual high wears off, and these believers start to panic out of fear that their faith is disappearing or that they were never a real Christian in the first place. But faith isn't fundamentally a feeling. Faith is the decision to trust and follow Jesus Christ, and it need not ebb and flow based on how emotionally charged we feel.

Personality can be a factor too. Just as certain people are more susceptible to particular diseases, some temperaments—especially those that tend to be melancholy or contemplative—are more vulnerable to questions and doubts.

Doubt also tends to develop among those who have been emotionally scarred from an experience in their past. If as children they were abused, if they were abandoned by their parents or spouse, if they've felt unloved by those people most important to them, they may develop chronic uncertainty about God. Deep down inside they may be fearfully waiting for God to let them down in the same way that people in their lives have.

Or our doubts can stem from the volitional part of life, from our will and the choices we make that hamper our relationship with God. Deliberate patterns of sin inevitably create a lack of peace and a sense of being separated from God. So when people can't find peace, they wonder why God isn't comforting them. When they feel God is distant, they begin to question whether God is there at all. Yet the whole time the underlying cause of their doubt is their own willful choice to cling to sin.

And there's no question that doubt will sweep through you like wildfire if you've never actually made the decision to commit your life to Christ. Maybe you're living on a hand-me-down faith from your parents, or maybe you believe you're a Christian because you were baptized as a child, you attend church, or you are in general agreement with Christian doctrine. But the Bible is clear: each one of us needs to make the choice to receive the free gift of forgiveness and eternal life that Christ is offering. When we do that, we're adopted into God's family, and we begin a relationship with him that will draw us closer and closer to him over time.

Step #2: ASK God and Others for Help.

Be as honest with God as was the father whose son was gripped by evil. "I do believe," he said to Jesus. "Help me overcome my unbelief!" (Mark 9:24). Actually, as we've defined it, the father wasn't suffering from unbelief, but he was afflicted with doubt. However, the key is this: *he asked Jesus to help him—and Jesus did.* Jesus healed the man's son. And, in the process, I'm sure he cured the man's unbelief as well.

Turn to God for help not as a last resort, but as a first priority. Ask him to lead you to answers, to provide you with insight, to give you wisdom, and to bolster your confidence in him. Tell him of your desire for a strong and vibrant faith.

Then turn to Christians in your life. It is so important for each of us, as followers of Christ, to be part of a small circle of friends who encourage each other to be authentic in our faith and to grow spiritually. James said we should honestly admit our struggles and shortcomings to each other and pray for one another. Why? So, James said, that we "may be healed" (James 5:16).

I've found that it's particularly helpful to seek out people who have a strong Christian faith themselves. In a sense, their faith is contagious, so we benefit when we hang around people who have a deep and abiding belief in the Lord Jesus. They tend to anchor us and reassure us, and we can always learn from the spiritual practices that they have integrated into their life to help them build a doubt-resistant faith.

Step #3: IMPLEMENT a Course of Treatment.

Once you've found the root cause of your doubt and sought help from God as well as from godly friends, you're in a better position—with their assistance—to identify and implement a strategy for fighting the doubt virus.

For instance, instead of just concluding that you have some vague intellectual concerns about Christianity, take the time to write down the specific questions you have. This exercise will help you zero in on exactly what's troubling you. Then, as you address your particular issues, you'll be surprised by how many resources are readily available to help you pursue satisfying answers.

Or perhaps you've determined that emotional issues are generating germs of doubt. Maybe an appropriate course of action would be to discuss them with a wise Christian friend, a pastor, or a counselor who can assist you in resolving them.

Or if your doubt is a matter of your will, ask yourself specifically what you're holding back from God and whether doing so is worth the cost you're paying

Hope is only hope when

there's still some measure of the

unknown that lies ahead of us.

as a consequence. After all, the choice is yours: you can let deliberate disobedience plague you with unnecessary doubt and spiritual disconnectedness for the rest of your life, or you can submit your whole self to God and really start experiencing the adventure of authentic Christianity.

And if you're not certain that you have ever actually given your life to Christ, then make sure once and for all. Pray and earnestly ask Jesus to forgive your sins and to lead your life. Don't hold anything back from him. It's all right if this prayer turns out to be a recommitment, but once you've done this sincerely, put the issue to rest. The Bible assures us that when we humbly receive Christ's gift of salvation, we're forgiven for all of our sins and adopted into his family forever. We don't have to doubt our salvation anymore (John 1:12; Romans 6:23; 1 John 1:9, 5:13).

I should also acknowledge the role that Satan plays in spreading the doubt virus whenever and wherever he can. Jesus called him "the father of lies" (John 8:44) because of the way he whispers distortions in our ear to create mistrust of God and confusion about our faith. We shouldn't ignore the threat he poses, but we shouldn't become fixated on him either. James advised, "Submit yourselves, then, to God. Resist the devil, and he will flee from you" (James 4:7). And the apostle John reminded us, "You, dear children, are from God . . . [and] the one who is in you is greater than the one who is in the world" (1 John 4:4).

Diagnosing the root of your doubt, seeking help and counsel, and implementing a course of action will put you on the road to recovery. You may have to deal with some temporary relapses along the way, but the next step is also vital in warding off infections in the future.

Step #4: TAKE Scrupulous Care of Your Spiritual Health.
The human body is less susceptible to viruses when it's healthy, because then its immune system can fight off minor infections before they become serious. In a similar way, a strong faith is able to fight off the doubt virus before it gains a foothold and threatens to overwhelm your defenses. Just as a body is strengthened by good nourishment and regular exercise, your faith becomes stronger with both knowledge and action.

By knowledge, I mean getting serious about learning more about God and why you can trust him. That learning involves not only reading books *about* the Bible, but also studying the Bible itself in a consistent and systematic way.

And during your day-to-day actions, you can build up your faith by exercising it. We learn best by doing, and we learn best about the trustworthiness of God when we make the daily decision to pour out our hearts to him in prayer and submit our lives to him in order to intentionally stretch our faith. The apostle Paul said, "Whatever you have learned or received or heard from me, or seen in me—put it into practice. And the God of peace will be with you" (Philippians 4:9). As King David put it, you can taste and see for yourself that the Lord is good (Psalm 34:8).

When you do these things, then whenever doubt threatens, you'll find it much easier to draw strength from your knowledge of God and your personal experience with him.

"I may not know the answer to this particular question," you'll say. "But I have plenty of evidence that God is real, that the Bible proves itself reliable, and that my Savior cares about me. All of that gives me confidence that God has an answer for this question too. So I'm not going to panic or toss my faith out the window. I'm not going to get mired in despair or fall into disillusionment. Instead, I'm going to keep relying on God, because he has shown me over and over that my trust in him is well placed."

Step #5: HOLD Your Remaining Questions in Tension.
God's thoughts are higher than ours (Isaiah 55:8–9). We are finite people with limited minds, so we can't expect to understand everything about our unlimited God. Consequently, we are bound to encounter some mysteries that won't be resolved at least for the time being.

In many cases we'll get a better glimpse of an answer as we mature in our faith. But in some instances we'll have to wait for heaven, when we can finally raise our hand and say, "Jesus, I have a question that's been bothering me for a long time."

I know that I'll be raising my hand. I'm sure you'll be raising yours as well. That's okay, because we can be confident God will give us answers. Plus, we'll have all of forever to satisfy our curiosity!

Holding On to Hope

But between here and heaven we can say, "I may not have answers to every peripheral issue, but the answers I do have point me unmistakably toward God who is real, dependable, and a Father who loves me. Because of that, my faith can stay intact and my hope in God strong even while I have some unresolved issues."

That's not an irrational faith. Instead, that's dealing with our doubts responsibly by making an informed decision, supported by what lawyers call the preponderance of evidence, to suspend judgment for a season. It's a conclusion, based on all the available data, that God can be trusted. It's therefore permissible to take a wait-and-see attitude toward a troubling matter or two.

Actually, if we had 100 percent of the answers to 100 percent of our questions, there wouldn't be any room for faith at all. And hope is only hope when there's still some measure of the unknown that lies ahead of us. As Scripture puts it, "Faith is *confidence in what we hope for* and *assurance about what we do not see*" (Hebrews 11:1, emphasis mine). Also, Romans 8:24 says, "Hope that is seen is no hope at all. Who hopes for what they already have?"

In addition, remember this: we may feel perplexed by mysteries, but there is no mystery for God. He understands all. In *The Gift of Doubt*, Gary Parker said it well: "I may not have the answer to many questions, but I know the One who does."[10]

The apostle Paul also knew that One well. And even Paul, in spite of his vast knowledge, realized how little he knew. So when you're trying to maintain your sense of hope in the midst of spiritual doubt, turn Paul's words into a personal prayer:

> Lord, I can see and understand only a little about you now, as if I were peering at your reflection in a poor mirror, but someday I am going to see you in your completeness, face-to-face. Now all that I know is hazy and blurred, but then I will see everything clearly, just as clearly as you see into my heart right now.[11]

In the meantime, be encouraged by the words of Rufus Jones, a pastor who put it this way a century ago: "A rebuilt faith is superior to an inherited faith that has never stood the strain of a great testing storm. If you have not clung to a broken piece of your old ship in the dark night of the soul, your faith may not have the sustaining power to carry you through to the end of the journey."[12]

When you're feeling dizzy and disoriented because of doubt, remember that observation. As you emerge from your uncertainties, I believe that you will possess a hardier faith, a deeper faith, and a more resilient, enduring, and hope-filled faith than you did before it was put to the test.

CHAPTER SIX

The Hope of Heaven

In his great mercy [God] has given us new birth into a living hope . . . and into an inheritance that can never perish, spoil or fade. This inheritance is kept in heaven for you.

1 PETER 1:3–4

ON A MILD AUTUMN AFTERNOON WHEN I WAS IN FIFTH grade, my friend Bart and I were playing on the monkey bars after school. When it was time to go home, I headed south toward my house, and Bart and his little brother rode their bicycles west toward theirs. As they approached a busy highway, Bart's foot slipped off the pedal. He was unable to brake, and before he could regain control of his bike, it rolled directly into the path of an oncoming truck.

As his helpless brother held him in his arms, Bart's lungs filled with blood and he died.

On a bright and beautiful morning when I was twenty-seven years old, my dad was driving down the highway on his way to catch the commuter train, just as he did every weekday. Without warning, he had a massive heart attack and was dead before the car came to a halt at the side of the road.

Just a few years after that, my friend Frank got up in the middle of the night because he was feeling queasy. Since he was only in his mid-thirties, he didn't think this was anything more than indigestion. But he soon fell over dead, leaving behind a wife, a six-year-old son, and a four-year-old daughter.

As a journalist, I've seen hundreds of instances in which people embarked on a day that started routinely but ended tragically. They were victims of drunk drivers, muggers, drive-by shooters, carjackers, auto accidents, household mishaps, fires, medical anomalies, or airplane crashes. Each year six thousand people are killed just trying to cross the street!

I'm not trying to be unduly alarming. However, some people look at the average life span in the United States and behave as though it's guaranteed to them. It's not. I was awakened to this fact on a personal level not long after putting my trust in Christ.

I had been working as managing editor of a newspaper in Missouri and had taken our family to Chicago to visit my mother for a few days. Late that night, I got up feeling ill and promptly collapsed in tremendous pain.

My wife called the paramedics. As they were on their way, I was sprawled on the floor. My breathing was shallow; my pulse, erratic; my skin, pale. I was fighting to stay conscious and feeling an ominous numbness creep up my arms and legs.

This is it, I thought to myself. I figured I was going to die just like Bart, Frank, and my dad.

I'll admit it: I was scared. I didn't want to die. I wanted to see my children grow up. I wanted to live a long and happy life with Leslie. I had been a Christian for about eighteen months, though, and I knew with certainty that I could count on two things if I died: first, that God would watch over Leslie and the kids; and, second, that the moment I closed my eyes in death, I would reopen them in the presence of God.

I was confident that Jesus would put his arm around me and say to the Father, "I know this man. I love him, and he loves me. I've paid for every single sin he's ever

*Once the most important
issue of life is resolved—once
you're assured of spending
eternity in heaven with God—
then your whole outlook
toward life is transformed.*

committed. On the merits of what I did on the cross, he is washed clean of all wrongdoing, clothed in my righteousness, and therefore able to spend eternity in heaven."

I was in a win-win situation: if I lived, everything would be fine; and if I died, everything would still be fine. As Paul said, "For to me, to live is Christ and to die is gain" (Philippians 1:21). That gave me the kind of courage and hope I needed to cope with the crisis.

Obviously, I didn't die. After nearly a week in the hospital, during which doctors were never quite able to diagnose the malady that had stricken me, I was discharged and blessed to go on and experience lots of other bright and beautiful days. But sooner or later one day will be my last. Death still stalks me, just as it does you.

There's an old saying that only two things in life are certain: death and taxes. But while people might be able to fudge on their taxes, ultimately none of us cheats death. It is ugly, unnatural, and morbidly efficient.

Many people fear the end. One-third of Americans are so afraid of death that they are emotionally unable even to ponder their own demise. They fear the pain of death, the unknown, being separated from their loved ones, and the deterioration of their body. They just can't face it.

BENEFITS OF THE HOPE OF HEAVEN

IF THERE IS EVER A TIME WHEN WE NEED *HOPE*, IT IS when we face death. More and more people in our culture—both religious and nonreligious—are asking the same question Job asked thousands of years ago: "If someone dies, will they live again?" (Job 14:14). What more important question is there?

Maybe that's why Paul said to his fellow believers in Christ, "Brothers and sisters, we do not want you to be uninformed about those who sleep in death, so that you do not grieve like the rest of mankind, *who have no hope*" (1 Thessalonians 4:13, emphasis mine).

That's also why I love what Jesus said to Martha after the death of Lazarus, who was her brother and Jesus' good friend: "I am the resurrection and the life. The one who believes in me will live, even though they die" (John 11:25).

In effect, Jesus was saying, "There *is* life after death. In fact, I'll prove it by bringing Lazarus back to life after he's spent four days in a tomb. I'll also prove it by returning to life after my own crucifixion, by appearing not just for a fleeting moment, but for forty days in order to convince the world that I did in fact rise from the dead. And because I will conquer the grave, my followers will too. They can be confident that they will reside with me for eternity in heaven."

That satisfies me. It gives me hope. And it gets me excited about our eternal future. In fact, let me offer three great things the hope of heaven does for us as Christians.

1. The Hope of Heaven Establishes Our Value.

The existence of heaven assures me that we really do matter to God. From cover to cover the Bible shouts this message: *God cannot stand the thought of spending eternity without us, his children.*

Think of that. The God of the universe—who could spend eternity any way he desires and with anybody or any being he chooses to create—wants to spend it with you and me. Doesn't that tell you something about how much you're worth to God? Doesn't that give you a new perspective of your value as a person?

I was reflecting on this while I was watching the Discovery Channel awhile back. They were showing a nature film about a family of ducks, and it showed the mother duck paddling around a pool with her twelve cute little ducklings.

After the swim, the mother hopped onto the cement

lip of the pool and began waddling away, and the babies lined up to follow her. The first one jumped up, but he plopped back down into the water. So he tried harder and jumped higher, made it up over the lip, and began following his mom. Then the second one jumped up and the third, and so on, all falling in line behind their mother.

But the twelfth little duckling tried jumping up and only made it two-thirds of the way before falling back into the pool. So he swam around a little, then jumped again, but again only made it halfway. He was getting frantic, flapping his little wings. He kept jumping and falling. It was clear he wasn't going to make it.

Guess what the mother duck did? I'm sorry to say that she just kept on walking. The narrator explained dispassionately, "The mother will abandon that duckling because it's probably too weak to survive. That sounds cruel, but that's the way nature is."

Have you ever felt that way—that you're too morally weak, that your spiritual efforts fall too far short, that you don't matter enough to God to warrant his concern? That when you stumble in sin, God is going to keep walking and not turn back to help you?

Thankfully, the Bible portrays God as the Good Shepherd who has one hundred sheep, but when just one of them gets left behind, he doesn't give up on it. Rather, he launches an all-out search to find that wayward sheep and then, once found, he carries it in his arms back home (Luke 15:4–7).

"The Lord is not slow in keeping his promise . . . Instead he is patient with you," Peter assured us, "not wanting anyone to perish, but everyone to come to repentance" (2 Peter 3:9). I thank God he didn't abandon me during those years when I rebelled against him. I thank God he didn't leave me behind when I fouled up and fell far short of his standards. I thank God he was patient with me, and that he's patient with you too.

That patience speaks volumes about how valuable we are to him.

2. The Hope of Heaven Bolsters Our Courage.

Second, the reality of heaven can help us be more courageous.

In his book *Surprise Endings*,[1] Ron Mehl recounted a story about a seventy-eight-year-old minister who was hired by a church in California. Not long after his arrival, the church members began to complain that he wasn't what they wanted. He wasn't a great speaker. He didn't have much pizzazz.

But instead of lovingly discussing their concerns with him, the congregation opted for guerrilla warfare. They talked during his sermons, they withheld their giving, they belittled him behind his back, and many people stopped attending. Sure enough, he soon got the message. And because he didn't want to hurt the church, he quietly resigned.

As he was leaving, two seminary students walked up to him. "So," they said, "what are you going to do? You don't have any family, you don't have any money, you don't have a home. Where will you go?"

This humble man of God replied without hesitation, "I'm going to heaven."

"Well, of course, we know that," they chortled. "But what are you really going to do? You have nowhere to turn and no one to help you."

"I'm going to heaven," he replied. "And the fact that I'm going to heaven makes these times of temporary hardship seem insignificant."

You see, once the most important issue of life is resolved—once you're assured of spending eternity in heaven with God—then your whole outlook toward life is transformed. There are still setbacks, there's still pain, there's still turmoil, and there's still tragedy, but you view those events from an entirely higher plane.

It's incredible to see what the apostle Paul endured for his faith. He was whipped with thirty-nine lashes on five different occasions; he was beaten with a rod three times; he was shipwrecked three times; he was nearly stoned to death; he was deprived of food, water, and clothing. Yet he declared in Romans 8:18, "I consider that our present sufferings are not worth comparing with the glory that will be revealed in us."

What a perspective! Whatever would happen to him between here and there, he knew that heaven was waiting, and that knowledge gave him incredible courage.

Can you say what Paul said? If today were one of those bright and beautiful days that suddenly brought a life-and-death crisis, would you have the confidence that comes from knowing that your eternity with God is secure?

The hope of heaven can give you that kind of courage.

3. The Hope of Heaven Ignites Our Excitement for the Future.
When your ultimate future is secure, you can be filled with an exciting sense of anticipation for what lies ahead.

One of the most wonderful times of anticipation I remember as a child was Christmas Eve. I would go to bed, but I was so excited that it would take me what seemed like forever to finally get to sleep. Then, in the morning, my sister Lorena and I would get up at the crack of dawn and crouch at the top of the stairs. While the rest of the family got ready to go down, we'd gaze at all the beautifully wrapped presents under the tree.

Here's the thing: We didn't know what the presents were going to be, but we knew that our mom and dad loved us and had spent a lot of time and effort choosing the exact gifts that would make us happy.

That's a bit like the sense of anticipation I feel about heaven. I don't know a lot of details about what heaven will be like. But I do know this: I have a heavenly Father who loves me, and I know he has spent a lot of time and effort creating an environment that will be custom-tailored to give me joy.

It's difficult for us to understand a lot about heaven because of our limited perspective. How can time-bound people comprehend the eternal? How can people from a world of sin and pain imagine a heaven without those things? Because of our limited knowledge of heaven, we tend to lose that vision and become mired in things down here.

Heaven won't be a place of isolation, loneliness, and alienation. Instead, we will enjoy rich and deep relationships in a community that shares the common treasure of Christ.

C. S. Lewis addressed this when he said, "We are half-hearted creatures, fooling about with drink and sex and ambition when infinite joy is offered us, like an ignorant child who wants to go on making mud pies in a slum because he cannot imagine what is meant by the offer of a holiday at the sea."[2]

The Bible puts it more poetically: "No eye has seen, no ear has heard, no mind has conceived what God has prepared for those who love him" (1 Corinthians 2:9).

Look at it this way. First think of all the wonderful things that ordinary people have created despite their limited intellect, their finite resources, and their sin-encumbered minds. There are hot fudge sundaes. The space shuttle. Ferrari convertibles. The US Constitution. Disney World. The Eiffel Tower. Harley Davidson motorcycles. The Autobahn. iPhones and iPads. La-Z-Boy recliners. Starbucks Frappuccinos. NBA basketball. The Golden Gate Bridge. Chicago-style hot dogs . . . and deep dish pizzas.

Not a bad list!

Now think about this: God has unlimited intellect, he has infinite resources, and he is unencumbered by sin. Plus, he's the One who gave us the creativity and resources necessary to create the items in the above list in the first place. Who *knows* what delights he's dreaming up for us to enjoy for all of eternity!

The Bible gives us only some hints, and they're tantalizing. For instance, heaven won't be a place of isolation, loneliness, and alienation. Instead, we will enjoy rich and deep relationships in a community that shares the common treasure of Christ. There will be loving and trust-filled friendships characterized by optimum rapport instead of the suspicion and distrust that often plague our relationships here.

And Jesus told us heaven will be like home. Specifically, He said, "My Father's house has many rooms; if that were not so, would I have told you that I am going there to prepare a place for you? And if I go and prepare a place for you, I will come back and take you to be with me that you also may be where I am" (John 14:2–3).

Do you know how it feels to travel for a long time, live in hotels in strange cities, and then finally get home? It feels great, right? Well, heaven will be the kind of home you've always longed for, a home where there's security, acceptance, love, and belonging, all custom-designed for you.

Again, C. S. Lewis was poignant when he reflected on

this sense of longing: "If I find in myself a desire which no experience in this world can satisfy, the most probable explanation is that I was made for another world."[3]

Heaven will also be untainted by sin. No more of the fear that permeates our lives and prompts us to lock our doors and look at strangers with suspicion. And if you're like me, you have lots of regrets over the way your sin has hurt others. Yet heaven is a place without regrets, without blame, without guilty consciences. It's a place where we make right choices, take appropriate actions, and build one another up instead of tear each other down.

The Bible says heaven will be a place where we're comforted and made whole, a place beyond pain and disabilities. God himself "'will wipe every tear from [our] eyes. There will be no more death' or mourning or crying or pain, for the old order of things has passed away" (Revelation 21:4).

Heaven will be a place where we'll worship and serve God out of an overwhelming sense of awe, wonder, and love, and we will never get bored. Remember, God is infinite, so we could spend all of eternity eagerly exploring him and his nature and never come to the end of getting to know him better. We'll be constantly thrilled by his majesty, glory, and greatness.

"You make known to me the path of life," Psalm 16:11 assures us. "You will fill me with joy in your presence, with eternal pleasures at your right hand." Who *knows* what that joy will be like? And who knows what those eternal pleasures will be? I think they'll involve adventure, growth, and excitement as we finally live the way God always intended us to live.

Then there's the ultimate experience when we finally see Jesus face-to-face. "Dear friends, now we are children of God, and what we will be has not yet been made known," 1 John 3:2 tells us. "But we know that when Christ appears, we shall be like him, for we shall see him as he is."

I have an unshakable confidence that when that day comes, I will look Jesus in the eye and he will reach out to lovingly enfold me in his arms. And if you know him, you can confidently look forward to that kind of a warm welcome as well.

The apostle John reinforced this confidence: "I write these things to you who believe in the name of the Son of God so that you may *know* that you have eternal life" (1 John 5:13, emphasis mine).

God has invited you personally to experience heaven with him. What have you done in response to that invitation? If you know you've received the forgiveness, leadership, and friendship of Christ, then you can enjoy an unsinkable sense of hope for the life ahead.

If you're unsure of where you stand with God, you may be wondering, "What's the price of admission?" I want to tell you as clearly as I know how that the cost is too steep for you to ever pay on your own. You can't buy your way into heaven by trying to be good. You can't earn your way in by being religious. The Bible says that all of our efforts fall short of God's standards (Romans 3:23).

The Bible also tells us that our wrongdoing separates us from God, so we need to somehow deal with those sins. We need to admit them, to turn away from them with God's help, and to receive Christ's payment for them by his death on the cross. In short, we need to receive his full forgiveness as a free gift of grace.

When you reach out to Jesus in prayer and wholeheartedly receive the grace he offers you, then you too can have full confidence that when your eyes close in death, they will reopen immediately in God's presence. You can live with the confident expectation, assurance, and joy that you'll spend eternity in heaven with Jesus and countless fellow believers, your brothers and sisters in Christ.

I can't think of a greater reason for hope than that!

The Lord himself will come down from heaven, with a loud command, with the voice of the archangel and with the trumpet call of God, and the dead in Christ will rise first. After that, we who are still alive and are left will be caught up together with them in the clouds to meet the Lord in the air. And so we will be with the Lord forever. Therefore encourage one another with these words.

1 THESSALONIANS 4:16–18

CHAPTER SEVEN

Hope for Every Person

You were separate from Christ . . . without hope and without God in the world. But now in Christ Jesus you who once were far away have been brought near by the blood of Christ.

EPHESIANS 2:12–13

WHY HAS GOD GIVEN US HOPE?

There are at least two reasons. The first is that he loves us as individuals and in ways that go far beyond our full comprehension. The Bible explains that "God demonstrates his own love for us in this: While we were still sinners, Christ died for us" (Romans 5:8). He sees us as highly valuable, worthy of rescue, and ideal recipients of his grace and affection. I hope you've reached the point of embracing his love for you, his friendship, and his leadership in your life—or that you will very soon.

But God's love doesn't stop with you and me. In fact, the best known verse in the Bible is John 3:16, and it tells us that "God so loved *the world* that he gave his one and only Son, that whoever believes in him shall not perish but have eternal life" (emphasis mine).

This truth leads to the second reason God has given us hope: he wants to work through us to tell *everyone* about his compassion and grace. He wants people around the world to understand that he is patient, "not wanting anyone to perish, but everyone to come to repentance" (2 Peter 3:9). He wants to invite them, like us, to receive his forgiveness, guidance, and adoption into his family.

So where do you and I fit into that divine enterprise? Well, he wants us to become distributors of his grace. He wants us to be so filled with faith, hope, and love that we can't help but let those blessings overflow into the lives of the people around us. He gave to us, in part, so that we will turn around and give to others. The apostle Paul put it this way: God "reconciled us to himself through Christ *and gave us the ministry of reconciliation* . . . We are therefore Christ's ambassadors, as though God were making his appeal through us" (2 Corinthians 5:18, 20, emphasis mine).

That appeal is to be extended even to the people in our lives who, for a variety of reasons, seem beyond the reach of God's love and hope. They may be coworkers, classmates, family members, or friends, but somehow we just can't imagine these individuals humbling themselves and following Christ. Perhaps they lack both the time and motivation to consider the Savior. They're firmly in charge of their own lives, and they seem bent on keeping it that way.

"Unlikely candidates" I call them. I understand the temptation to give up on these folks; I'm sometimes tempted to do the same.

That is, until I remember what an unlikely candidate *I* once was. I know that I too lived much of my life, as Ephesians 2:12 puts it, "without hope and without God in the world." Thankfully, as the passage continues, I was one who, though "far away," was "brought near" by God (v. 13).

When I think about that, I realize anew that if God could reach down and rescue someone like *me*, he can reach down and rescue pretty much *anybody*.

"That sounds good," you might say, "but you don't know *my* friend. He has lived such a wild and rebellious life that I don't think he could *fathom* what it would be like to let God turn his life around!" Or "She is so self-centered and strong-willed that she seems incapable of admitting

Maybe if we renew our hope in God, increase our vision for the people around us, pray more earnestly on their behalf, extend his grace in ways least expected . . . we would begin to see God work in them in ways that we currently cannot even ask or imagine.

she needs help of any kind." Or "This particular family member is simply too set in his ways to ever allow anything or anyone to change him." Or "She's been hurt so badly by someone who claimed to be a Christian that she's not at all interested in God or church."

While I can sympathize with that sort of skepticism, let me remind you that God has supernatural strength, unfailing love, and extraordinary patience—and that he delights in doing miracles in people's lives. The gospel remains "the power of God that brings salvation to everyone who believes" (Romans 1:16). It's still true that "the arm of the LORD is not too short to save, nor his ear too dull to hear" (Isaiah 59:1). And he is the God who is "able to do immeasurably more than all we ask or imagine" (Ephesians 3:20).

Maybe if we renew our hope in God, increase our vision for the people around us, pray more earnestly on their behalf, extend his grace in ways least expected, and speak more boldly into their lives, we would begin to see God work in them in ways that we currently cannot even "ask or imagine."

And while it's true that I don't know your friends or what they're up against, I do know my own friends, many of whom started out as unlikely candidates just like me.

Remember former gang member Ronnie Bronski and how God worked in his life? Maybe hearing how God reached and redeemed a few of my other friends would help bolster your hope for the people you know—and maybe even your hope for yourself.

Let's begin with a man named Billy.

Hope for Lawbreakers

I was in the beautiful town of Rome, Georgia, near the foothills of the Appalachian Mountains. The morning was cool but sunny, and I got dressed and headed over to a nearby church for Sunday services.

Outside, politely greeting everyone with a handshake as they arrived, was William Neal Moore, looking sharp in a tan suit with dark stripes, a crisp white shirt, and a brown tie. His face was deep mahogany, and his black hair was close-cropped. What I remember most was his smile: it was at once shy and warm, gentle and sincere, winsome and loving. It made me feel welcome.

"Praise the Lord, Brother Moore!" declared an elderly woman as she grasped his hand briefly and then shuffled inside.

Moore is an ordained minister at the church, which

is sandwiched between two housing projects in a racially mixed community. He is a devoted husband, a doting father, a faithful provider, a hard-working employee, and a man of compassion and prayer who spends his spare time helping hurting people whom everyone else seems to have forgotten. In short, Brother Moore is a model citizen.

But turn back the clock to May 1984. At that time, Moore was locked in the deathwatch cell at the Georgia State Penitentiary, down the hallway from the electric chair where his life was scheduled at one point to be snuffed out in less than seventy-two hours.

This was not the case of an innocent man being railroaded by an overly aggressive justice system. Unquestionably, Moore was a murderer. He had admitted as much. After a childhood of poverty and occasional petty crimes, he had joined the Army and later became depressed by marital and financial woes. One night he got drunk and broke into the house of a seventy-seven-year-old man named Fredger Stapleton who was known to keep large amounts of cash in his bedroom.

From behind a door, Stapleton let loose with a shotgun blast, and Moore fired back with a pistol. Stapleton was killed instantly, and within minutes Moore was fleeing with $5,600. An informant tipped off the police, and the next morning Moore was arrested at his trailer outside of town. Caught with the proceeds from the crime, he admitted his guilt and was summarily sentenced to death. He had squandered his life and turned to violence, and now he would face his own violent end.

This was a man without hope—at least from a human perspective.

However, the William Neal Moore who was counting down the hours to his execution was not the same person who had murdered Fredger Stapleton. Shortly after Moore was imprisoned, two church leaders visited him at the behest of his mother. They told him about the mercy and hope available through Jesus Christ.

"Nobody had ever told me that Jesus loves me and died for me," Moore explained to me later that Sunday. "It was a love I could feel. It was a love I wanted. It was a love I *needed*."

After hearing this life-giving message from those two men, Moore said yes to Christ's free gift of forgiveness and eternal life, and he was promptly baptized in a small tub that was used by prison trustees.

William Neal Moore would never be the same.

For sixteen years on death row, Moore was a missionary among the other inmates. He led Bible studies and conducted prayer sessions. He counseled prisoners and introduced many of them to faith in Jesus Christ. Churches sent people to visit him on death row—and be counseled by him! He took dozens of Bible courses by correspondence.

Moore even won the forgiveness of his victim's family. He became known as "The Peacemaker" because his cell block, largely populated by inmates who had become Christians through his influence, was always the safest, the quietest, and the most orderly.

Meanwhile, Moore inched closer and closer to execution. Legally speaking, his case was a hopeless cause. Since he had pleaded guilty, there were virtually no legal issues that might win his release on appeal. Time after time, the courts reaffirmed his death sentence.

So profound was the depth of his transformation, however, that more and more people outside the prison began to take notice. Mother Teresa and others started campaigning to save his life. "Billy's not what he was then," said a former inmate who had met Moore in prison. "If you kill him today, you're killing a body, but a body with a different mind. It would be like executing the wrong man."[1]

Praising Moore not only for being rehabilitated but also being "an agent of the rehabilitation of others," an editorial in the *Atlanta Journal and Constitution* declared "In the eyes of many, he is a saintly figure."[2]

Just hours prior to Moore being strapped into the electric chair, shortly before his head and right calf would be shaved so that the lethal electrodes could be attached, the court surprised nearly everyone by issuing a temporary halt to his execution.

Even more amazing, the Georgia Board of Pardons and Paroles later voted unanimously to spare his life by commuting his sentence to life in prison. After that, what was *really* astounding—in fact, unprecedented in modern Georgia—was when the Board of Pardons and Paroles decided that Moore, an admitted and once-condemned armed robber and murderer, should go free. On November 8, 1991, he was released on parole.

As I sat with Moore in his home overlooking a landscape of lush pine trees, I asked him about the source of his amazing metamorphosis.

"It was the prison rehabilitation system that did it, right?" I asked.

Moore laughed. "No, it wasn't that," he replied.

"Then it was a self-help program, or simply maintaining a positive mental attitude," I suggested.

He shook his head emphatically. "No, not that either."

"Prozac? Transcendental Meditation? Psychological counseling?"

We can't be filled with the power of God until we let go of the pretense that we can get by on our own.

"Come on, Lee," he said. "You know it wasn't any of those."

He was right. I knew the real reason. I just wanted to hear him say it. "Then what was responsible for the transformation of Billy Moore?" I asked.

"Plain and simple, it was Jesus Christ," he declared adamantly. "He changed me in ways I could never have changed on my own. He gave me a reason to live. He helped me do the right thing. He gave me a heart for others. He saved my soul."

That's the power of Jesus to change a human life and to bring hope where there was none before. As the apostle Paul wrote, "If anyone is in Christ, the new creation has come: The old has gone, the new is here!" (2 Corinthians 5:17).

Billy Moore the Christian is not the same as Billy Moore the killer. God intervened with his forgiveness, with his mercy, with his power, and with the abiding presence of his Spirit. That same transforming grace is available to everyone who acts on the message of Jesus Christ by turning away from their sin and embracing him as their Forgiver and Leader.

There really is hope for all who are willing to say yes to God and his ways.

HOPE FOR THE PROUD

Robert got his thrills by living on the edge, taking extraordinary risks, and dramatically cheating death. His life was awash in alcohol and one willing woman after another. He made mountains of money and then gambled much of it away. He once settled a dispute with a business associate by using a baseball bat, and that landed him in jail. So he rode to the jail in a stretch limousine, served his time, and then rode back home again in the same limo.

Robert was the quintessential narcissist. At the height of his success, he owned two private jets, which cost thousands of dollars an hour to operate. One day he ordered both of them into the air. Why? He wanted to sit inside one of them, sip expensive champagne, and look out the window at the other one flying in tandem. He wanted to see his name emblazoned on his other jet's tail as they soared through the sky!

Robert didn't hate God. In a way, the situation was worse than that. At least despising God would have required a measure of thought or emotion. Instead, God was simply irrelevant to him. Unnecessary. A nonissue.

To Robert, God's name was only a swear word. He belittled people for their faith in Jesus Christ. And all the while he seemed to make it a hobby to go out and break God's commandments—that were there for his own good. Robert lived his whole life this way. For sixty-five years he reveled in his rebellion against God and, really, worshipped only the god of himself.

Then one spring day Robert was walking along the beach near his home in Florida when something extra-ordinary happened: he heard God speak to him. Not out loud, but internally. He actually sensed God saying, *Robert, I've rescued you more times than you'll ever know. Now I want you to come to me through my Son Jesus.*

Robert was shocked. Why was God, out of the blue, speaking to him? And who was Jesus—really? Robert wasn't at all sure. So he called a friend who was a Christian and started asking him questions. The friend suggested he get my book *The Case for Christ*, which he did and sub-sequently read cover to cover. In response to the prayers of Robert's daughter and her church, God was touching Robert directly by the Holy Spirit.

"All of a sudden I just believed in Jesus Christ. I did! I believed in him!" Robert remembered with wide-eyed enthusiasm. "I just got on my knees and prayed that God would put his arms around me and never, ever, ever let me go."

At that moment, Robert began to change in ways that only God's Spirit could accomplish. His hardened heart softened. His selfishness began to dissolve. His priorities were turned upside down. He couldn't do enough for God. He became as passionate about his relationship with Christ as anyone I have ever encountered.

In fact, Robert wanted to tell the world that his life had changed and that he was now a follower of Jesus Christ. So he asked the pastor of a large church he had seen on TV to baptize him and to let him say a few words about his experience with God.

When Robert was baptized, he told his story with such simplicity, such emotion, and such childlike conviction that there wasn't a dry eye in the sanctuary. One by one, God began stirring in the hearts of his listeners that morning. Throughout the church God was whispering, "Now is the time for you too."

When the pastor—who decided to jettison his sermon because, he explained, Robert had already given the best sermon—asked if anyone else wanted to receive Christ and be baptized, something amazing happened. Men and women, young and old, began streaming toward the platform. First ten, then twenty, then a hundred. . . . Then two hundred. . . . Then three hundred. . . . Ultimately about *seven hundred* people, accompanied by the song "Amazing Grace," came forward during the two services.

Amazing grace indeed.

I became friends with Robert after he called to thank me for writing my book. Since we lived on opposite coasts, we would chat over the phone, usually every other week or so. He was constantly asking me theological questions, and he was always eager to learn more about God and the Bible. His biggest regret, Robert told me, was that he hadn't surrendered his life to Jesus when he was much younger. So he would challenge me, saying, "Lee, you have to tell people, 'Don't put this off! *Don't* put it off!'" And I'd hear in his voice this sense of remorse that he couldn't go back and live those earlier years over.

"There's just so much I want to do for God," he told me again and again.

Time, however, was running out for Robert. He was suffering from a lung condition that had plagued him for years, and just a few months later he died. When they buried him near his childhood home in Montana, thousands of people flocked to his funeral.

You might wonder, "Why would so many people

want to honor a guy like Robert?" That's a natural question to ask, but only because I haven't told you the rest of the story. You see, nobody called Robert by his real name; they always referred to him instead by his nickname, which was *Evel*.

This unlikely Christian, known by the name *Evel Knievel*, risked his life to jump motorcycles over increasingly challenging obstacles, in the process landing in the *Guinness World Records* book for breaking more bones than any other human being.[3] Unexpectedly, extraordinarily, this once self-absorbed celebrity had been humbled and awed by God's undeserved love.

So while thousands of admirers flocked to his memorial service to pay tribute to Evel, his tribute went somewhere else. Before he died, Evel had asked for these words to be etched on his tombstone for all the world to see: "Believe in Jesus Christ".

Hope for the Resistant

I'll confess that I was always a little afraid of Leslie's dad, my father-in-law. The rough-hewn product of Cicero, Illinois (Capone's old stomping grounds, he often reminded me), Al was a stout, brusque, and fiercely opinionated barber who found his niche later in life shearing hair at a military base. When you got through his tough-as-nails exterior, you'd find a heart of gold, but it wasn't always easy to bore through that armored shell.

Still, we did enjoy one thing we had in common: we were both satisfied atheists—until Leslie became a follower of Jesus. Then, two years later, I did as well. One of the first things I said to Leslie after I became a Christian was, "We should tell Al about this!"

The very next time we got together, in a burst of naive enthusiasm, I excitedly told Al the story of my spiritual journey. My unstated implication was, *Hey, Al, you should become a Christian too!*

Al listened, but his expression remained stoic. "Look, that's fine for you," he said, jabbing a finger at me to punctuate his point. "But don't ever bring up Jesus to me again, okay?"

To his credit, through the years that followed, Al never criticized or tried to impede or inhibit my faith in any way. In fact, when I later told him with great trepidation that I was going to leave my newspaper career and take a 60 percent pay cut to work at a church, he surprised me with his supportiveness. "If that's what you feel you want to do with your life," he said, "then you should do it."

For the next twenty years, all Leslie and I could do for Al was authentically live out our faith and pray for him each day. Honestly, I don't think we missed many days that whole time. Yet throughout those years we saw in Al not one glimmer of interest in spiritual matters. His language remained just as coarse; his skepticism toward church never softened; and his indifference toward God was always complete.

Then one day Al suffered a stroke. Leslie and I huddled with his doctor at the nurse's station outside Al's hospital room. After going through an elaborate medical explanation that neither of us quite understood, the doctor gave this ominous prognosis: "Al is going to have a series of these strokes over the next several months until one of them is fatal."

When Al was released from the hospital, Leslie and I moved him and his wife, Helen, who was a Christian, to a house that was close to ours. Al became increasingly lethargic. We avoided the uncomfortable topic of his diagnosis, never coming out and explicitly discussing his condition with him. It was simply understood that Al was slowly fading away.

Finally, I couldn't take it anymore. I had to talk to my father-in-law about his need for Christ. So one day

I encouraged Leslie and Helen to go out shopping so Al and I could be alone. After they left, I pulled up a chair to face Al, who was seated in a recliner in his living room.

"Al," I said with intensity. "Do you realize you're dying? Do you understand that you don't have much longer in this world?"

Al looked at me with sadness in his eyes, but he didn't say anything.

"I don't want to be in heaven without you. Leslie and Helen and the grandkids—none of us want to be in heaven without you. *Please*, Al," I pleaded.

Still, there was no response.

"Al, you can be in heaven with all of us. Jesus paid the price for your sins. If you admit your wrongdoing— and, Al, you know you haven't always lived the way you should—then you can receive Christ's forgiveness for everything you've ever done wrong. He will wipe your slate clean and open the door to heaven for you. It's a free gift, Al. Why wouldn't you want to receive it?"

I could tell Al was tracking my every word, but he remained silent. I didn't know what else to say, and that's when I did something I had never done before, something that seemed so very needed at the moment.

I sat back in my chair and whispered under my breath

so that Al, who was hard of hearing, couldn't make out what I was saying: "Satan, unhand him! Let him go! He is *not* yours!" I felt like the evil one actually had Al in his grasp and was going to drag him away.

I turned back to Al and continued to implore him to receive Jesus. I explained repentance as best I could. I emphasized that despite his best intentions to live a good life, he was a sinner who needed God's grace. And slowly I began to see a crack in Al's facade. Something in his face told me that his heart was opening.

"Al, you want to confess your sins and receive Christ right now, don't you?" I asked—and then I held my breath.

Instantly, tears filled his eyes, and Al slowly nodded. I breathed a sigh of relief, and then I led him, sentence by sentence, through a simple prayer of repentance and faith. The whole time my heart felt like it was going to explode!

At the end, a smile played at the corner of Al's mouth. I went over and hugged him like never before. "Welcome home, Al!" I declared. "Welcome home."

Almost on cue, Leslie and Helen returned from shopping, and I told them the great news. They erupted in celebration, and Al beamed as they hugged and kissed him.

It was time for a spiritual birthday party! Leslie started to cook a special dinner, but after a little while, we noticed that something was wrong with Al. His right side was suddenly weak. "He's having another stroke!" Leslie screamed.

We called 9-1-1, and the paramedics loaded him into an ambulance. Leslie climbed inside, while I drove with Helen to the hospital in our car. The ambulance arrived first. As they began wheeling Al into the emergency room, he looked up at Leslie and said softly, "Tell Lee thanks."

It turned out that this stroke was the one that would destroy Al's mind. He was left in a state of constant confusion. Al lingered for several weeks . . . and then he finally went *Home.*

So, in the last cogent conversation of his life and after more than eighty years of ardent atheism, Al Hirdler— one of the people I had most struggled to hold out hope for—finally opened his heart to God's gift of outrageous grace.

Al discovered hope . . . just in time.

Hope for Your Friends

THINK AGAIN ABOUT THOSE FRIENDS AND FAMILY MEM-bers in your life who seem beyond God's reach. Have they engaged in crimes worse than the murder and theft committed by Billy Moore? Are they more self-centered and full of pride than Evel Knievel, who squandered millions of dollars on self-aggrandizement and reckless living, all the while shaking his fist at God? Are they more spiritually stubborn and aloof than Al Hirdler, who denied God's existence and spurned his grace for more than eight decades?

I didn't think so. But even if they were, as Paul explained in Romans 5:20, "Where sin increased, grace increased all the more."

Listen, friend: Nobody—not the most rebellious, resistant, or irreligious person you've ever met, and certainly not you—no one is beyond the reach of God's grace.

"These three remain: *faith, hope and love,*" God reminds us (1 Corinthians 13:13), and they're available to *everyone* who will humble themselves enough to simply reach out and receive him.

THE SUM OF THE MATTER

I TRUST YOU'VE ENJOYED OUR JOURNEY THROUGH *THE Case for Hope*. We've endeavored to understand what genuine, biblical hope is and then to learn how to live it out in our own lives.

Nobody — not the most rebellious,

resistant, or irreligious person you've

ever met, and certainly not you — no one

is beyond the reach of God's grace.

We've sought to anchor that hope in the historical events surrounding Jesus' resurrection. His rising from the dead proved that he is who he claimed to be—the Son of God—and that he has the credentials and the authority necessary to offer us salvation, a gift that impacts us in this life and the next.

We explored how God can transform our lives and how he will give us the power we need to live for him both today and into the future.

Next, we saw how we can cling to hope even in—perhaps *especially* in—the times of doubt. And we learned how to embrace the hope of heaven and saw how that hope can benefit our lives in important ways.

Finally, we renewed our hope in God's life-changing power, made available not only to us but also to our most spiritually distant friends, by recounting the stories of three unlikely candidates who were revolutionized by God's grace.

What's left? Well, I'm now going to step out of the way and encourage you to take a journey in which you allow God's Word to speak to you in very personal and direct ways.

Specifically, I've put together for you a 30-Day Journey of Hope in the following pages.

Chapter Eight

A 30-Day Journey of Hope

We have this hope as an anchor for the soul, firm and secure.

Hebrews 6:19

We've looked at the topic of hope from a variety of angles, and we've referenced a number of Bible verses along the way. My prayer is that this approach has been informative as well as encouraging to you.

But often the best thing we can do is to focus on Scripture itself and let it speak to us directly or, more accurately, to let *God* speak to us directly through his written Word.

Colossians 3:16 admonishes us to "let the word of Christ dwell in you richly." So in the spirit of that passage,

I've laid out thirty Bible passages that speak in various ways on the topic of hope. I encourage you to begin a "30-Day Journey of Hope" in which you meditate daily on one specific passage of Scripture and *let God's words of hope dwell in you richly.*

Then, after reflecting on the passage and asking God to guide your response, write down the thoughts that come to your mind and any action steps you feel God may be leading you to take. Close with a prayer related to what you've sensed God has impressed upon you that day. To make this experience even richer, encourage a friend, your small group, or a class at your church to do this 30-day journey with you.

I'm confident that this experience will deepen your grasp of hope as well as your gratitude to God for it. May he bless you on your journey!

Journey of Hope – Day 1

God will never forget the needy; the hope
of the afflicted will never perish.

Psalm 9:18

_____

_____

_____

_____

_____

_____

_____

_____

_____

_____

_____

_____

_____

_____

_____

_____

_____

_____

JOURNEY OF HOPE – DAY 2

*The eyes of the LORD are on those who fear him, on
those whose hope is in his unfailing love . . . We wait in
hope for the LORD; he is our help and our shield.
In him our hearts rejoice, for we trust in his holy name.
May your unfailing love be with us, LORD,
even as we put our hope in you.*

PSALM 33:18, 20–22

_____

_____

_____

_____

_____

_____

_____

_____

_____

_____

_____

_____

_____

Journey of Hope – Day 3

Why, my soul, are you downcast? Why so disturbed within me?
Put your hope in God, for I will yet praise
him, my Savior and my God.

Psalm 42:5

_____

_____

_____

_____

_____

_____

_____

_____

_____

_____

_____

_____

_____

_____

_____

_____

JOURNEY OF HOPE – DAY 4

Yes, my soul, find rest in God;
my hope comes from him.

PSALM 62:5

_____

_____

_____

_____

_____

_____

_____

_____

_____

_____

_____

_____

_____

_____

_____

_____

_____

_____

JOURNEY OF HOPE – DAY 5

You have been my hope, Sovereign LORD,
my confidence since my youth.

PSALM 71:5

_____

_____

_____

_____

_____

_____

_____

_____

_____

_____

_____

_____

_____

_____

_____

_____

Journey of Hope – Day 6

*You are my refuge and my shield; I have
put my hope in your word.*

Psalm 119:114

_____

_____

_____

_____

_____

_____

_____

_____

_____

_____

_____

_____

_____

_____

_____

_____

_____

JOURNEY OF HOPE – DAY 7

*Anyone who is among the living has hope—even a
live dog is better off than a dead lion!*

ECCLESIASTES 9:4

_____

_____

_____

_____

_____

_____

_____

_____

_____

_____

_____

_____

_____

_____

_____

_____

_____

_____

Journey of Hope – Day 8

*Those who hope in the LORD will renew their
strength. They will soar on wings
like eagles; they will run and not grow weary,
they will walk and not be faint.*

ISAIAH 40:31

_____

_____

_____

_____

_____

_____

_____

_____

_____

_____

_____

_____

_____

_____

_____

_____

_____

Journey of Hope – Day 9

This is what the LORD Almighty says: "Do not listen
to what the prophets are prophesying to you; they
fill you with false hopes. They speak visions
from their own minds, not from the mouth of the LORD."

JEREMIAH 23:16

_____

_____

_____

_____

_____

_____

_____

_____

_____

_____

_____

_____

_____

_____

_____

Journey of Hope – Day 10

*"For I know the plans I have for you," declares
the Lord, "plans to prosper you and not to harm
you, plans to give you hope and a future."*

Jeremiah 29:11

_____

_____

_____

_____

_____

_____

_____

_____

_____

_____

_____

_____

_____

_____

_____

_____

_____

_____

JOURNEY OF HOPE – DAY 11

*Since we have been justified through faith, we have peace
with God through our Lord Jesus Christ, through whom we have
gained access by faith into this grace in which we now stand.
And we boast in the hope of the glory of God.*

ROMANS 5:1–2

_____

_____

_____

_____

_____

_____

_____

_____

_____

_____

_____

_____

_____

_____

_____

JOURNEY OF HOPE – DAY 12

We ourselves, who have the first fruits of the Spirit,
groan inwardly as we wait eagerly for our adoption
to sonship, the redemption of our bodies.
For in this hope we were saved.

ROMANS 8:23–24

_____

_____

_____

_____

_____

_____

_____

_____

_____

_____

_____

_____

_____

_____

_____

_____

_____

JOURNEY OF HOPE – DAY 13

*Never be lacking in zeal, but keep your
spiritual fervor, serving the Lord.
Be joyful in hope, patient in affliction, faithful in prayer.*

ROMANS 12:11–12

_____

_____

_____

_____

_____

_____

_____

_____

_____

_____

_____

_____

_____

_____

_____

_____

_____

*Everything that was written in the past was written to teach us,
so that through the endurance taught in the Scriptures
and the encouragement they provide we might have hope.*

ROMANS 15:4

_____

_____

_____

_____

_____

_____

_____

_____

_____

_____

_____

_____

_____

_____

_____

_____

_____

Journey of Hope – Day 15

May the God of hope fill you with all joy
and peace as you trust in him,
so that you may overflow with hope by
the power of the Holy Spirit.

Romans 15:13

_____

_____

_____

_____

_____

_____

_____

_____

_____

_____

_____

_____

_____

_____

Journey of Hope – Day 16

I pray that the eyes of your heart may be enlightened in order that you may know the hope to which [God] has called you, the riches of his glorious inheritance in his holy people, and his incomparably great power for us who believe.

Ephesians 1:18–19

_____

_____

_____

_____

_____

_____

_____

_____

_____

_____

_____

_____

_____

_____

_____

_____

_____

*There is one body and one Spirit, just as you were
called to one hope when you were called; one Lord, one
faith, one baptism; one God and Father of all,
who is over all and through all and in all.*

EPHESIANS 4:4–6

_____

_____

_____

_____

_____

_____

_____

_____

_____

_____

_____

_____

_____

_____

_____

Journey of Hope – Day 18

*We always thank God, the Father of our Lord Jesus Christ,
when we pray for you, because we have heard of your faith in
Christ Jesus and of the love you have for all God's people—the
faith and love that spring from the hope stored up for you in
heaven and about which you have already heard in the
true message of the gospel that has come to you.*

Colossians 1:3–6

_____

_____

_____

_____

_____

_____

_____

_____

_____

_____

_____

_____

_____

Journey of Hope – Day 19

[God] has reconciled you by Christ's physical body through death to present you holy in his sight, without blemish and free from accusation—if you continue in your faith, established and firm, and do not move from the hope held out in the gospel.

Colossians 1:22–23

_____

_____

_____

_____

_____

_____

_____

_____

_____

_____

_____

_____

_____

_____

_____

Journey of Hope – Day 20

We remember before our God and Father
your work produced by faith,
your labor prompted by love, and your endurance
inspired by hope in our Lord Jesus Christ.

1 Thessalonians 1:3

_____

_____

_____

_____

_____

_____

_____

_____

_____

_____

_____

_____

_____

_____

_____

Journey of Hope – Day 21

Brothers and sisters, we do not want you to be uninformed about those who sleep in death, so that you do not grieve like the rest of mankind, who have no hope.

1 Thessalonians 4:13

_____

_____

_____

_____

_____

_____

_____

_____

_____

_____

_____

_____

_____

_____

_____

_____

JOURNEY OF HOPE – DAY 22

*May our Lord Jesus Christ himself and God our
Father, who loved us and by his grace gave us eternal
encouragement and good hope, encourage your hearts
and strengthen you in every good deed and word.*

2 THESSALONIANS 2:16–17

_____

_____

_____

_____

_____

_____

_____

_____

_____

_____

_____

_____

_____

_____

_____

_____

JOURNEY OF HOPE – DAY 23

Command those who are rich in this present
world not to be arrogant nor to
put their hope in wealth, which is so uncertain,
but to put their hope in God,
who richly provides us with everything for our enjoyment.

1 TIMOTHY 6:17

JOURNEY OF HOPE – DAY 24

We wait for the blessed hope—the appearing of the glory of our great God and Savior, Jesus Christ, who gave himself for us to redeem us from all wickedness and to purify for himself a people that are his very own, eager to do what is good.

TITUS 2:13–14

_____

_____

_____

_____

_____

_____

_____

_____

_____

_____

_____

_____

_____

_____

_____

Journey of Hope – Day 25

Let us hold unswervingly to the hope we profess,
for he who promised is faithful.

Hebrews 10:23

_____

_____

_____

_____

_____

_____

_____

_____

_____

_____

_____

_____

_____

_____

_____

_____

Journey of Hope – Day 26

*Faith is confidence in what we hope for
and assurance about what we do not see.*

HEBREWS 11:1

_____

_____

_____

_____

_____

_____

_____

_____

_____

_____

_____

_____

_____

_____

_____

_____

Journey of Hope – Day 27

Praise be to the God and Father of our Lord Jesus Christ! In his great mercy he has given us new birth into a living hope through the resurrection of Jesus Christ from the dead, and into an inheritance that can never perish, spoil or fade. This inheritance is kept in heaven for you.

1 Peter 1:3–4

_____

_____

_____

_____

_____

_____

_____

_____

_____

_____

_____

_____

_____

JOURNEY OF HOPE – DAY 28

With minds that are alert and fully sober, set
your hope on the grace to be brought to you when
Jesus Christ is revealed at his coming.

1 PETER 1:13

_____

_____

_____

_____

_____

_____

_____

_____

_____

_____

_____

_____

_____

_____

_____

_____

JOURNEY OF HOPE – DAY 29

*In your hearts revere Christ as Lord. Always be
prepared to give an answer to everyone who asks you
to give the reason for the hope that you have.
But do this with gentleness and respect.
Since we have such a hope, we are very bold.*

1 PETER 3:15; 2 CORINTHIANS 3:12

_____

_____

_____

_____

_____

_____

_____

_____

_____

_____

_____

_____

_____

_____

JOURNEY OF HOPE – DAY 30

Dear friends, now we are children of God,
and what we will be has not yet
been made known. But we know that when Christ
appears, we shall be like him, for we shall see him
as he is. All who have this hope in him
purify themselves, just as he is pure.

1 JOHN 3:2–3

_____

_____

_____

_____

_____

_____

_____

_____

_____

_____

_____

_____

_____

The Case for Hope

Endnotes

Chapter One

1. Douglas Colligan, "That Helpless Feeling: The Dangers of Stress," *New York*, July 14, 1975, 28, cited by Charles R. Swindoll, *Man to Man* (Grand Rapids: Zondervan, 1996), 65.

2. Arnold Hutschnecker, *Hope: The Dynamics of Self-Fulfillment* (New York: Putnam, 1981), 33.

3. "Pollster Gallup Feels Spirit Traveling All Over the World," *Chicago Tribune*, August 1, 1986, includes the first part of the quote. The quote in its entirety can be found in Lee Strobel, *What Jesus Would Say* (Grand Rapids: Zondervan, 1994), 159.

4. "Most Americans (74%) believe in life after death," according to a Pew Research report on "U. S. Religious Landscape Survey: Religious Beliefs and Practices," June 1, 2008, accessed January 11, 2015, http://www.pewforum

.org/2008/06/01/u-s-religious-landscape-survey-religious
-beliefs-and-practices.

Chapter Two

1. Charles Colson said this in a speech video that Steven Curtis Chapman showed as part of his live performance of the song "Heaven in the Real World" at the GMA Dove Awards program, April 28, 1994.

2. Bertrand Russell, "A Free Man's Worship" in *The Basic Writings of Bertrand Russell*, eds., Robert E. Egner and Lester E. Denonn (New York: Simon and Schuster, 1961), 67.

3. Damon Linker, "Where are the honest atheists?" *TheWeek.com*, March 8, 2013, accessed January 11, 2015, http://theweek.com/article/index/241108/where-are-the -honest-atheists#axzz342GsQEmo.

4. Ven. S. Dhammika, *Good Questions Good Answers*, "What or where is Nirvana?" accessed January 11, 2015, www .buddhanet.net/ans22.htm.

5. All quotations of the Qur'an are from www.quran.com. Accessed January 11, 2015.

6. The full version of my interview with Michael Licona can be found in Lee Strobel, *The Case for the Real Jesus* (Grand Rapids: Zondervan, 2007).

7. Gary R. Habermas and Michael R. Licona, *The Case for the Resurrection of Jesus* (Grand Rapids: Kregel, 2004).

8. John Dominic Crossan, *Jesus: A Revolutionary Biography* (San Francisco: HarperCollins, 1991), 145.

9. James D. Tabor, *The Jesus Dynasty: The Hidden History of Jesus, His Royal Family, and the Birth of Christianity* (New York: Simon & Schuster, 2007), 230 (emphasis in original).

10. Jesus was executed in AD 30 or 33.

11. Dean John Rodgers of Trinity Episcopal School for Ministry, quoted in Richard N. Ostling, "Who was Jesus?" *Time*, August 15, 1988.

12. See Josephus (Ant. 20:200); Hegesippus (quoted by Eusebius in EH 2:23); Clement of Alexandria (quoted by Eusebius in EH 2:1, 23).

13. William Ward, *Christianity: A Historical Religion?* (Valley Forge, PA: Judson, 1972), 93–94.

14. To read some of the broader evidence for Jesus' resurrection, see Lee Strobel, *The Case for Christ: A Journalist's Personal Investigation of the Evidence for Jesus* (Grand Rapids: Zondervan, 1998).

15. William Lane Craig, *Assessing the New Testament Evidence for the Historicity of the Resurrection of Jesus* (Lewiston, NY: Edwin Mellen, 1989), 420.

16. In Jeremiah 29:11, God makes a promise to his people *then* that can have application in the lives of his people *now*.

17. Rick Warren, *The Purpose Driven Life* (Grand Rapids: Zondervan, 2002, 2012).

18. Rick Warren, "The Answer Is Easter: Find Hope This Easter with Pastor Rick Warren," accessed January 11, 2015, www.youtube.com/watch?v=MLv0NUnkCyU.

CHAPTER THREE

1. John Newton, "Amazing Grace" (emphasis mine). Public domain.

CHAPTER FOUR

1. *National Geographic News*, "Flash Facts About Lightning," June 24, 2005, accessed February 3, 2015, http://news .nationalgeographic.com/news/2004/06/0623 _040623_lightningfacts.html.

2. "Average Daily Global Lightning Strikes," July 8, 2005, accessed February 3, 2015, http://www.newton.dep .anl.gov/askasci/wea00/wea00239.htm.

3. Ole Hallesby, *Prayer* (Minneapolis: Augsburg, 1994), 23.

4. You can read his story in *God's Smuggler* by Brother Andrew and John and Elizabeth Sherrill (Grand Rapids: Chosen, 1967, 2001).

5. Brother Andrew with Verne Becker, *The Calling* (Nashville: Moorings, 1996), 26–27.

CHAPTER FIVE

1. My thinking about this has been greatly influenced by Gary R. Habermas and his books *Dealing with Doubt* (Chicago: Moody, 1990) and *The Thomas Factor: Using Your Doubts to Draw Closer to God* (Nashville: Broadman & Holman, 1999).

2. C. S. Lewis, *Mere Christianity* (New York: Macmillan, 1952), 123.

3. Os Guinness, *In Two Minds: The Dilemma of Doubt and How to Resolve It* (Downers Grove, IL: InterVarsity, 1976), 25.

4. Karl Barth, *Evangelical Theology: An Introduction* (New York: Holt, Rinehart, and Winston, 1963), 124.

5. Lynn Anderson, *If I Really Believe, Why Do I Have These Doubts?* (Minneapolis: Bethany House, 1992), 25–26.

6. Gary R. Habermas, *Dealing with Doubt* (Chicago: Moody, 1990), 15.

7. Again, my thinking here has been strongly influenced by Gary Habermas and his books on doubt.

8. Mark R. Littleton, "Doubt Can Be a Good Thing," *The Lookout* (March 17, 1991), 5.

9. R. C. Sproul, ed., *Doubt and Assurance* (Grand Rapids: Baker, 1993), 24.

10. Gary E. Parker, *The Gift of Doubt: From Crisis to Authentic Faith* (San Francisco, Harper & Row, 1990), 142.

11. Based on 1 Corinthians 13:12 in *The Living Bible*.

12. Rufus Jones, *The Radiant Life*, quoted in Parker, *The Gift of Doubt*, 71.

CHAPTER SIX

1. Ron Mehl, *Surprise Endings: Ten Good Things About Bad Things* (Sisters, OR: Multnomah, 1995).

2. C. S. Lewis, *The Weight of Glory* (New York: HarperCollins, 2001), 26.

3. C. S. Lewis, *Mere Christianity* (New York: HarperCollins, 2001), 136–137.

CHAPTER SEVEN

1. Bill Montgomery, "U. S. Supreme Court Halts Execution: Even Victim's Family Pleaded for Mercy," *Atlanta Journal and Constitution*, August 21, 1990.

2. "When Mercy Becomes Mandatory," *Atlanta Journal and Constitution*, August 16, 1990.

3. *Guinness World Records*, accessed January 11, 2015, www.guinnessworldrecords.com/records-11000/most-broken-bones-in-a-lifetime.

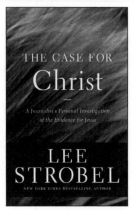

The Case for Grace

A Journalist Explores the Evidence of Transformed Lives

Lee Strobel, New York Times Bestselling Author

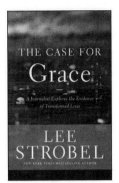

The Case for a Creator explored the scientific evidence for God;

The Case for Christ investigated the historical evidence for Jesus;

The Case for Faith responded to eight major objections about Christianity;

The Case for The Real Jesus refuted the current challenges to the Bible and Christ ...

Now, in *The Case for Grace*, Lee Strobel crafts a compelling and highly personal account about grace, focusing on God's transforming work in the lives of men and women today.

With unusual candor, Lee draws upon his own journey from atheism to Christianity to explore the depth and breadth of God's redeeming love for spiritually wayward people. He travels thousands of miles to capture the inspiring stories of people whose values have been radically changed and who have discovered the "how" and "why" behind God's amazing grace. You'll encounter prodigal sons, addicts, and even murderers who have found new hope and purpose. You'll meet once-bitter people who have received God's power to forgive those who have harmed them—and, equally amazing, people mired in guilt who have discovered that they can even forgive themselves.

Through it all, you will be encouraged as you see how God's grace can revolutionize your eternity and relationships.

The Search for Grace

"[God] waits to be wanted. Too bad that with many
of us He waits so long, so very long, in vain."
—A.W. TOZER

HE WAS LEANING BACK IN HIS LEATHER RECLINER IN the wood-paneled den, his eyes darting back and forth between the television set and me, as if he didn't deign to devote his full attention to our confrontation. In staccato bursts, he would lecture and scold and shout, but his eyes never met mine.

It was the evening before my high school graduation, and my dad had caught me lying to him—big time.

Finally, he snapped his chair forward and shifted to look fully into my face, his eyes angry slits behind his glasses. He held up his left hand, waving his pinky like a taunt as he pounded each and every word: *"I don't have enough love for you to fill my little finger."*

He paused as the words smoldered. He was probably expecting me to fight back, to defend myself, to blubber or apologize or give in—at least to react in some way. But all I could do was to glare at him, my face flushed. Then after a few tense moments he sighed deeply, reclined again in his chair, and resumed watching TV.

That's when I turned my back on my father and strode toward the door.

I didn't need him. I was brash, I was driven and ambitious—I would slice my way through the world without his help. After all, I was about to make almost a hundred dollars a week at a summer job as a reporter for a rural newspaper in Woodstock, Illinois, and live on my own at a boarding house.

A plan formulated in my mind as I slammed the back door and began the trek toward the train station, lugging the duffel bag I had hurriedly packed. I would ask the newspaper to keep me on after the summer. Lots of reporters have succeeded without college, so why not me? Soon I'd make a name for myself. I'd impress the editors at the Chicago papers and eventually break into the big city. I'd ask my girlfriend to move in with me. I was determined to make it on my own—and never to go back home.

Someday, there would be payback. The day would come when my father would unfold the *Chicago Tribune* and his eye would catch my by-line on a front-page exclusive. That would show him.

I was on a mission—and it was fueled by rage. But what I didn't realize as I marched down the gravel shoulder of the highway on that sultry June evening was that I was actually launching a far different quest than what I had supposed. It was a journey that I couldn't understand back then—and which would one day reshape my life in ways I never could have imagined.

That day I embarked on a life-long pursuit of grace.

———

Thus begins my book *The Case for Grace: A Journalist Explores the Evidence of Transformed Lives*. I traveled thousands of miles to interview people with amazing stories that each added a piece to the puzzle of grace.

I found inspiration and insights in the life of a Korean orphan, shivering under straw in a foxhole; in a teenage addict in Amarillo who didn't care whether his next injection would kill him; in a homeless felon in Las Vegas, scouring dumpsters for scraps of pizza crust; in a humiliated pastor in South Carolina, unmasked for his hypocrisy; in the famous preacher's son who was living a wasted and vapid life in Boston; and in a Cambodian man who fled the Khmer Rouge, only to find his life intertwined with a notorious war criminal.

I wrote *The Case for Grace* to encourage and strengthen the faith of Christians, but also to point anyone who is spiritually curious to the amazing message of God's love for each of us – regardless of the path our lives have taken so far. To get this message to the younger generation, we simultaneously produced *The Case for Grace for Kids* and *The Case for Grace Student Edition.*

This was my most difficult book to write. When you read it, you'll see why—I talk very candidly about my difficult relationship with my father, some awful mistakes I made when I was an atheist, and how a brush with death caused a crisis in faith. Though these were often painful episodes to discuss, my hope is that they will point readers to the God who stands ready to forgive us, adopt us, and transform us.

I resonate with the apostle Paul's words in Acts 20:24: "I consider my life worth nothing to me; my only aim is to finish the race and complete the task the Lord has given me—the task of testifying to the good news of God's grace." With this book, you'll have a way to breathe fresh life into your faith—and perhaps new life into others.

LEE STROBEL